D1413066

Praise From Readers

An Hasidic anecdote states: "It is not within our power to place the divine teachings directly in someone else's heart. All we can do is place them on the surface of the heart so that when the heart breaks, they will drop in." *Spirituality in Recovery* compassionately targets hearts open to the spiritual life because of the brokenness of addiction. It is a book full of practical suggestions and concrete steps. The content rings true with the wisdom of ones for whom the spiritual life is a living reality, a road they have travelled for themselves and others.

— Mark E. Deihl, MS, NCC
Associate Pastor for Congregational Care
First Presbyterian Church
Nashville, TN

Spirituality in Recovery very eloquently addresses the recovering person's great need for simplicity and "walking around" spiritual principles. A tremendously useful addition to recovery literature.

— James Luna, NCAC
Counselor, Cumberland Heights
Nashville, TN

A dynamic and powerful book which offers a penetrating model for healing the frustration, emptiness, and despair within the heart and mind.

Those suffering from addictive and/or compulsive behaviors will recognize the walls and barriers which separate them from God and the abundance of spiritual blessings.

This book will enable readers to confront the issues of living life within an imperfect world while striving for the attainment of spirituality.

It is must reading for the recovering person who is hurting, confused, and searching for inward peace from God.

— *LaRue Moss, Ph.D.*
Director of The Counseling Ministry
Woodmont Hills Church
Nashville, TN

Powerful in its simplicity. Practical. Helpful.

— *George Allen, NCACII*
Nashville, TN
NADAC Counselor of the Year

I understood the meaning of spirituality for the first time after reading this book. I am grateful for its existence and recommend it to all my friends in recovery.

— *Jim L.*
Nashville, TN

Spirituality in Recovery plunges into the CORE issues of successful recovery. The book describes 12 basic human emotions that often trip one to stumble and fall into relapse, and provides the spiritual formula of how to transform these into new positive power-emotions of successful recovery. It is a must-read book for everyone in recovery.

— Dr. Bill Anderson
Host, RecoveryLine
Clinical Psychologist

Spirituality in Recovery is the most comprehensive, yet simple and understandable work, I have ever read on this most difficult aspect of recovery.

— Harold Gilliland
New Life Lodge
Burns, , TN

Here is a straightforward approach to spirituality that will help the person faced with the brokenness of addiction. Thank you for sharing it with me and the many others who will read and profit from it.

— Bud Brainerd
Senior Minister, Memorial Presbyterian Church
Montgomery, AL

SPIRITUALITY
IN
RECOVERY
A 12 Step Approach

Paul Barton Doyle
&
John Ishee

ISBN: 0-939298-37-6

PRINTED IN THE UNITED STATES OF AMERICA

NEW DIRECTIONS
A Division of
JM Productions
P. O. Box 1911
Brentwood, TN 37024-1911
Phone:(615) 373-4814
FAX: (615) 373-8495
Toll Free: 1-800-969-READ

CONTENTS

Acknowledgments

To mentors:

My wonderful family, Barbara, Jennifer, Chelsea, and Alana for constant love and support.

George Allen, for helping me to more clearly understand acceptance, even though I don't practice it enough.

Ed Counter, L. C. Batson, Elaine Willers, Mack Hargis Billy Escue, Franklin Jones, and Andrew Poston for their support and encouragement throughout my career.

LaRue Moss, who serves as an unending source of courage and inspiration, for her steadfast confidence

And most of all,

My grandmother, Evelyn Strange, my first mentor and role model, who has practiced unconditional love and acceptance even in the face of extraordinary circumstances.

— Paul Doyle

Acknowledgments

To:

My devoted family, Myra and Mark, for their unending support and help.

Cumberland Heights Alcohol and Drug Treatment Center for allowing me to serve as pastoral counselor during the past eight years.

The 6,000 plus patients with whom it has been my privilege to counsel while in treatment. Thank you for your trust.

—John Ishee

Introduction

Since you have decided to read this book, we think you should know a little about how and why we wrote it. First, be aware that it was not written in a hurry. It did not spring full grown from our heads, as Greek mythology alleges that Athena sprang from the head of Zeus. It cames from years of practical "hands on" experience of working with recovering persons.

Our first book, *In Step With God*, made explicit the fact that the 12 steps were biblically based. This volume is a natural sequence to the first book. It focuses on maintaining conscious contact with God.

We have sought in this book to provide a workable process for practicing 12 step spirituality, allowing each person to bring his or her own beliefs to the process. Each chapter contains descriptive material and activities that an individual can use to enhance conscious contact with God. The closing pages provide guidelines for using the book in groups.

We have written primarily to persons in recovery from mood-altering chemicals, but the information should also be helpful to people with other compulisve behaviors.

Finally, we wish there was a singular pronoun that indicated both male and female. Since there is not, we ask the reader to bear with us as we often use the masculine gender, as is traditional. Of course, we all know that addiction knows no gender.

The activities for each chapter are just as beneficial as the text itself. Your reading, digesting, and internalizing of the text is indeed important. The activities, however, are designed to take you one step further by providing opportunities for practice. In addition, recording your thoughts and ideas on separate paper can be helpful.

Working a personal recovery program is often exactly that—work. And work can sometimes be painful and frustrating. A maxim in recovery is "The program will work if you work it." We hope you will take this notion to its highest, that of *living* the program. Only as we internalize the essence of our spirituality will we begin to realize that God is doing for us what we cannot do for ourselves.

Paul Doyle   John Ishee

Prologue

We begin this odyssey in spirituality with three basic assumptions: (1) Each of us *is* a spiritual person. God has created us in His image. That means that we *are* spiritual beings. Thus, it is not our purpose to help you to *become* "spiritual." Rather, our intent is to help you *improve* the quality of your spirituality. (2) Addiction *diminishes* the quality of one's spirituality. The addicted person becomes preoccupied with the mood-altering chemical and the lifestyle associated with it. Thus, there is a feeling of alienation from God. (3) Recovery involves spiritual awakening. For some people that awakening is an initial experience; for others it is a return to the God of their understanding. For others, still, it is the beginning of a new quest in spirituality in which they experience God in new and different ways. Regardless of the nature of one's beliefs, the most important factor is summed up in Step 11: *Sought through prayer and meditation to improve our conscious contact with God as we understood God, praying only for the knowledge of God's will for us and the power to carry that out.*

You have made us for yourself, O God, and our hearts are restless until we find rest in you.

—Augustine

Something there is that doesn't love a wall, that wants it down.

—Robert Frost

The spiritual life is not a theory. We have to live it.

—Alcoholics Anonymous, p. 83

1

Spirituality:
The Power and the Process

For several years, Sam had a growing awareness that he had an alcohol and drug problem. At first, he denied it. "I drink too much sometimes, and sometimes I take pills," he said, "but I can quit anytime I want to." As his drinking continued, family members and friends continued to tell him that he needed help. "Maybe I do have a problem," he finally admitted, "but I can control it."

During the weeks and months that followed, Sam tried. Most of the time, however, his efforts were futile. His intention to take only one or two drinks resulted in his getting completely out of control. That's when Sam realized that he could not control his drinking through his own efforts.

Then came the anger. He was sometimes angry at

himself; sometimes angry at family members, blaming them for his problems; and sometimes angry at God, asking "Why?"

Things went from bad to worse. Sam's wife threatened to leave him. His children avoided him. His boss confronted him about his absenteeism and lack of productivity on the job.

Fortunately, the company for whom Sam worked provided an employee assistance program. Sam went to see the employee assistance counselor and was admitted to an alcohol treatment center for help.

In treatment, Sam was confronted with many of his compulsive and addictive thought patterns and behaviors. He found it helpful, even though it was sometimes painful to look at himself and to try and change.

Sam was made aware of the 12 step program and how to follow it to a sober and happy lifestyle. He could not help but notice the emphasis on spirituality — and it was a pleasant surprise.

Approximately one out of 10 people in our culture will at some time in their lives have a problem with mood altering chemicals.

Approximately one out of 10 people in our culture will at some time in their lives become addicted to mood altering chemicals. Some of them will need the help of a treatment center; others will be able to establish sobriety through the 12 step program, which is used effectively not only for alcoholics, but for other behavioral disorders.

The Twelve Steps

We encourage you to take a close look at the 12 steps to discover how spirituality is emphasized. Seven out of the 12 steps make direct or indirect reference to spiritual things. Actually, if all references to spirituality were removed from the 12 steps, it would be a bleak program indeed.

Examine the 12 steps as listed below. The bold type is our addition. We have added it to help you locate the references to spirituality. How many references can you find?

1.We admitted that we were powerless over alcohol — that our lives had become unmanageable.

2.Came to believe that **a Power greater than ourselves** could restore us to sanity.

3.Made a decision to turn our will and our lives over to the care of **God,** as we understood **God.**

4.Made a searching and fearless moral inventory of ourselves.

5.Admitted to **God,** to ourselves, and another human being the exact nature of our wrongs.

6.Were entirely ready to have **God** remove all these defects of character.

7.Humbly asked **God** to remove our shortcomings.

8.Made a list of all persons we had harmed, and became willing to make amends to them all.

9.Made direct amends to such people wherever possible, except when to do so would injure them or others.

10.Continued to take personal inventory and when we were wrong promptly admitted it.

11.Sought through **prayer and meditation** to improve our conscious contact with **God as we understood God**, praying only for the knowledge of **God's will for us** and power to carry that out.

12.Having had a **spiritual awakening** as the result of these steps, we tried to carry this message to alcoholics and to practice these principles in all our affairs.

Power comes from the spirituality that one experiences as the 12 steps are put to work in daily life.

Note that only steps 1, 4, 8, 9 and 10 do not have a direct reference to spirituality. However, the ideas implied in these steps involve spiritual activities and thoughts. If these were the only steps in the program, what kind of program would it be? Obviously, not a very powerful one. The power comes from the spirituality that one experiences as the 12 steps are put to work in one's daily life.

The Twelve Steps are reprinted with permission of Alcoholics Anonymous World Services, Inc. Permission to reprint and adapt the Twelve Steps does not mean that A.A. is in any way affiliated with this program. A.A. is a program of recovery from Alcoholism. Use of the Twelve Steps in connection with programs and activities which are patterned after A.A. but which address other problems does not imply otherwise.

The process that one goes through in working the 12 steps may be summarized as follows:

Step 1: Giving up: Surrender becomes the gateway through which we become willing to receive help from God and other people.

Step 2,3: Looking upward: Step 2 leads us through the process of rediscovering God or, for some people, discovering God for the first time. Step 3 calls for us to make a commitment to God as we understand Him.

Steps 4, 5, 6, 7: Looking inward: Step 4 leads us to make an inventory of ourselves. In Step 5 we share the inventory with another person, conscious of the fact that we are doing it in the presence of God. In Steps 6 and 7 we become ready for God to remove our defects of character and humbly ask Him to do so.

Steps 8,9: Looking outward: In Steps 8 and 9 we seek to make reconciliation with and amends to persons we have harmed through our compulsive behaviors.

Steps 10, 11, 12: Looking forward: The last three steps are maintenance steps, the means by which we continue to work the 12 step program.

The 12 step program originated as a program to help persons afflicted with the disease of alcoholism. Since its beginning, its application for other areas of life has become apparent.

More than 200 different kinds of groups use the 12 steps to focus on addictive or compulsive behavior.

More than 200 different kinds of groups use the 12

7

steps or some adaptation of them in support groups that focus on compulsive and/or addictive behaviors. While there are slight alterations in the 12 steps to make them explicitly applicable to varying groups, there is usually very little change in the steps as they relate to spirituality.

In essence, here is the spiritual message of the 12 steps. An individual with addictive or compulsive behavior admits that he is powerless over the situation. He comes to believe that the God of his understanding can help him. He makes a decision to surrender his will and his life to the care of God. After making a searching and fearless inventory of himself, he shares his findings with another person, conscious that he is doing so in the presence of God. He asks God to remove his defects of character. He seeks to make amends to persons he has harmed. He embarks on a lifelong pilgrimage of prayer and meditation to improve his conscious contact with God, praying only for the knowledge of his will and the power to carry that out. Finally, he seeks to carry the message of 12 step recovery to other persons and to practice the principles outlined in the 12 steps in all of his affairs.

---

12 step programs are not one-time events; rather, they are lifelong processes. A person never "completes" the programs.

Is there anyone who would not benefit from such a program? The answer is obvious. The 12 steps offer a process of spiritual growth that would be beneficial for anyone. They have been especially effective for persons seeking recovery from addictive and/or compulsive behaviors.

Thus, one can be proud of being a part of one of the greatest fellowships in the world—a fellowship of persons committed to growth in their lives through the practice of the 12 steps.

What is Spirituality?

Let's begin our definition of spirituality by eliminating some inadequate but often held views. First, 12 step spirituality is more than a set of beliefs or doctrines. Each of us has personal beliefs about God, but possessing such beliefs does not guarantee the practice of spirituality. No one completely understands God. As the Bible teaches, we see through a glass darkly...." To say that we do not completely understand God is not an encouragement toward ignorance; rather, it is a recognition that God is always more than each or all of us understand Him to be. He is God, and our understanding of Him is always based on the perceptions that emerge out of our experiences.

As the heavens are high above the earth, so are my thoughts higher than your thoughts and my ways higher than your ways (Isa. 55:9).

The 12 step program focuses on God as each person understands Him. That means at least two things—pluralism and tolerance. Pluralism means that there exists among persons in 12 step programs a wide diversity of beliefs. Tolerance means that each person should be allowed to enter and work the program without intimidation from other people who possess differing views.

Pluralism and tolerance serve as cornerstones for effective 12 step programs.

The following illustration should clarify what we mean when we refer to pluralism and tolerance.

For reasons of anonymity, the person shall remain nameless. He was from Iran and had come to this country to engage in graduate studies, but his studies were interrupted by his addiction. As he talked about his relationship with God, he sounded very much like the other patients who were of the Christian persuasion. He did not focus on specific beliefs about God; rather, he focused on his relationship with God.

When he finished his 28 day treatment program, he was presented a medallion as a memento of his time and effort in treatment. He came to John's office with a request. "I want you to bless this medallion," he said. For a moment, John was puzzled about how to respond. Then John reached out and clasped his hand in which the medallion was held. Together they prayed — a Moslem for Iran and a Christian minister for the United States — to the God and Father of all humankind for his blessings upon each of them. Such is the spirit of the 12 step program.

The 12 step program allows for diversity among the persons involved.

Since the 12 step program is used internationally, the concepts of God brought to the program are frequently products of the culture.

In the American culture, the greater percentage of people in 12 step programs come from a Christian heritage. Such does not imply that only persons of the Christian persuasion can find the 12 steps helpful. Neither does it imply that there is no place for Jesus Christ as one's Higher Power. A historical study of the 12 steps reveals that they grew out of the Christian heritage. Moreover, there is a great deal of similarity between the process one experiences as he works the 12 steps toward sobriety and what one experiences as he follows the scriptural teachings about coming into a right relationship with God.

As one continues to work the 12 step program, he will grow in his understanding of God, but spirituality is more than understanding.

Second, spirituality is not primarily a list of "dos" and "don'ts." Our moral and ethical behavior is greatly affected as we work the 12 steps, but our conduct grows out of a relationship with God, as we understand Him. Changes in our moral and ethical behavior occur as our relationship with God continues to grow.

Third, spirituality is more than a good feeling. As we maintain a positive relationship with God, we do experience positive feelings, but feelings and spirituality are not the same. If we assume that spirituality is the same as a good feeling, when we do not feel good we will have to assume that we are not spiritual — and that simply is not so.

Often, some of the most spiritually significant times in life are the times of suffering. During those times, God often comes to us in special ways. Scott Peck reminded us:

> It is in the whole process of meeting and solving problems that life has meaning. Problems are the cutting edge that distinguishes between success and failure. Problems call forth courage and our wisdom, indeed they create courage and wisdom. It is only because of problems that we grow mentally and spiritually. It is through the pain of confronting and resolving problems that we learn.[1]

Spirituality is more than a set of beliefs. It is more than a list of rules. It is more than a good feeling.

Spirituality is a personal relationship between an individual and God as that individual understands him. Out of that relationship beliefs emerge, morals and ethics improve, and feelings become more positive.

A Model to Help You Remember

The diagrams on the following pages illustrate how the relationship works.

We are body, soul (mind-emotion), and spirit. The spirit is the part of us that communicates with God and through which God communicates to us. The spirit is God-given. Each of us is a spiritual person, although we may not be making conscious contact with God each day.

Each of us is created to have a relationship with God. It is natural for us to do so. It is unnatural not to do so. But we often possess attitudes and engage in actions that cause us to feel alienated from God. This happens to people from all backgrounds, not just those who are addicted. But it almost always happens to addicted people. A wall of feelings emerges that alienates a person from God.

Before the relationship between a person and God can be re-established, the individual must own and deal with the feelings that are separating him from conscious contact with God.

The "wall" of feelings is illustrated and charted on the following pages. We can experience one or more of these feelings at the same time.

Negative feelings are best dealt with by taking action to replace them with positive ones. The positive feelings are listed on the chart on the following page. Study the chart carefully. How many of these feelings have you experienced? How many are you experiencing now? In the following chapters attention will be given to understand these feelings and taking action to change them into positive ones.

Notes

1. Scott Peck, *The Road Less Travelled* (New York: Simon and Shuster, 1978), p. 16

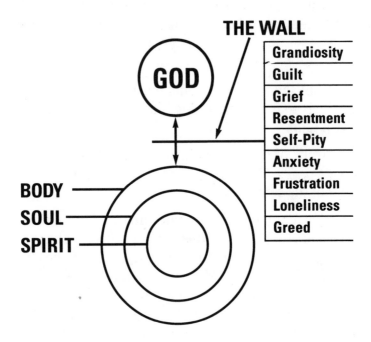

Spirituality is one's relationship with God. God has created us as spiritual beings, made to live in a positive relationship with Him. God is constantly available for us to experience Him. Negative attitudes and feelings, such as those listed above create a wall between us God. While such feelings are experienced by all people, they are experienced to a greater degree by addicted persons because of the painful circumstances that addiction creates.

The Wall of Feelings

Spirituality is our relationship with God, as we understand Him. We maintain that relationship through conscious contact. Negative feelings, which rob us of self-esteem, can be replaced with positive ones .

Grandiosity – A false feeling of superiority, a desire to be independent of God and others. The antidote is **humility.**	**Guilt** – A distressing feeling caused by violation of one's internal code of conduct. The antidote is **forgiveness.**	**Grief** – An emotional reaction resulting from a perceived loss. The antidote is **release.**
Resentment – "Cold" anger buried within a person as a result of being hurt or frightened. The antidote is **love and understanding.**	**Self-Pity** – A loss of gratitude for life. The antidote is **gratitude.**	**Anxiety** – A threatening feeling about one's ability to adequately deal with past, present or future events. The antidote is **security through faith.**
Frustration – The blockage of efforts to reach a goal... The antidote is **acceptance.**	**Loneliness** – The feeling of not being meaningfully connected to people or to God . The antidote is **intimacy.**	**Greed** – Preoccupation with efforts and desires to meet one's own needs. The antidote is **generosity.**

Negative feelings form a wall between us and God and cause us not to love ourselves, which prevents us from giving and receiving love from others and from God. Through our willingness, God's grace intervenes to help us grow and change negative feelings into positive ones .

15

TODAY

I asked God for strength that I might achieve; I was made weak that I might humbly learn to obey.

I asked for help that I might do great things; I was given infirmity that I might do better things.

I asked for riches that I might be happy; I was given poverty that I might be wise.

I asked for power that I might have the praise of men; I was given weakness that I might feel the need for God.

I asked for all things that I might enjoy life; I was given life that I might enjoy all things.

I asked for a vision that I might control my future; I was given awareness that I might be grateful now.

I got nothing I asked for but everything I had hoped for. Almost in spite of myself my unspoken prayers were answered.

I am among all people most richly blessed.

—Anonymous

2
From
Alienation
to
Conscious Contact

A little girl was in the front yard of her house playing with her doll. A plane flew over. "See the plane?" the little girl asked the doll. Of course, the doll did not answer. Then, in frustration, the little girl repeated, "See the plane?" Still there was silence. Finally, the little girl shook the doll and said, "I said, do you see the plane?" The little girl could see it, but the doll could not. And even if the doll could have seen it, it could not have spoken.

Legend holds that after Michelangelo had finished his sculpture of the biblical character, Moses, it appeared so lifelike that he commanded the statue to speak. When it did not speak, he threw an object at it.

How strange it is that people who have the privilege of

talking with God often act as dumb as a doll or as mute as Michelangelo's Moses.

Of all of God's creatures, we humans are the only ones who can talk to Him. What a marvelous opportunity we have! It deserves not to be neglected.

Prayer is conscious contact with God. It is not just talking to God, asking for things we want. Prayer is listening to ascertain what God would have us do to follow His will and expressing our desires to Him.

Through conscious contact with God the wall of separation between us and God begins to crumble. The re-establishment of this relationship (or, perhaps, the establishment of it for the first time) does not come totally from our efforts. God takes the initiative when we are willing for Him to do so. We only need to become ready and willing.

Basic Assumptions

Five basic assumptions about God can be helpful as we pray. *First, we must admit that we are not God.* The world does not revolve around us. We are not in charge. Recognizing this fact can change our perception of all that is around us. It is easy for the practicing alcoholic to admit that he is not God. After all, his guilt will not let him think otherwise. However, the sober alcoholic, having achieved some measure of success in putting life back in order may be sorely tempted to allow his ego to get out of control and to begin to play God.

Second, assume that God is. Several things affirm this belief. Yogi Berra said, "You can observe a lot of things just by looking." Look at the world—its existence, its order, its beauty, its wonder. Did such a world come into existence by accident? To think so is like believing that a tornado could hit a junk yard, blow debris around, and leave a super jet there, ready to fly. The probability of such is nil. It is easier to explain the world by believing in God than to try to explain it by some other means.

When you are willing to receive His revelation, God will reveal himself; He will become a reality to you in a way that you can receive it.

Third, assume that God, who created the world and us, loves us unconditionally. The term "unconditional love" is often used, but less often understood.

On occasions when we are trying to help recovering persons understand unconditional love, we will engage one person in the group in a conversation that goes something like this:

John: Sam, do you have children?

Sam: Yes, I have two boys, ages 6 and 9.

John: Sam, I am going to ask you a crazy question. Do you love your children?

Sam: Of course, I do.

John: Sam, I am going to ask you an even crazier question. Why do you love your children?

Sam: I just do. They are mine.

John: Right! You love your children because they are yours. Now, why does God love us?

Sam: Because we are His.

John: Do your children always do what you want them to do?

Sam: (laughing) I wish they did.

John: Sam, when your children fail to do what you want them to do, do you stop loving them?

Sam: Of course not.

John: Why?

Sam: Because I love them regardless of what they do.

John: Sam, that's unconditional love. That's the kind of love God has for us. We often hurt ourselves by our disobedience, but that does not stop God from loving us. The Bible uses a family relationship because that relationship best approximates how God loves us. He is our Father.

Fourth, assume that God wants what is best for us. He wants us to have a happy and meaningful life.

It makes no sense to say that God loves us unconditionally and then to say think that He wants us to be miserable.

God wants his children to find meaning in life. Some

people seem to have the notion that God sits in heaven taking great delight in making people miserable. Nothing could be further from the character of God as revealed in scripture.

Finally, assume that God is smarter than we are and knows how to help us to be happy better than we know ourselves. J. B. Phillips wrote an intriguing little book entitled *Your God Is Too Small.* He described how he asked people if they thought God knew anything about many of the modern inventions and discoveries. People's first responses often expressed doubt that God was that "up-to-date" in his understanding. Then, the people would say, "Yes, God knows everything." Science is discovering new things each year, but they are only discovering what God already knows and allows us to become aware of according to his schedule.

If we can assume that God loves us and is willing to help us, we will have little difficulty with turning our wills and our lives over to His care and maintaining conscious contact with Him.

How to Pray

Addicted people seldom think ill of God; they would rather not think of Him at all. To do so increases their feelings of guilt and shame. However, addicted persons do pray, usually when they are in distress. Their prayers are attempts to relieve the distress and desperation they feel. Prayers of this kind are usually attempts to bargain with God to find relief from distress. The scenario goes like this: "God, if you will help me, I promise to ____."

21

While bargaining with God is not the best response, it should not be discounted entirely. Many people began their road to recovery by such praying. However, bargaining with God usually does not turn out to be an experience that improves one's spiritual life.

There are three ways that a person can perceive how a bargain with God turns out. *First, one can conclude that "God did his part, but I did not do mine."* The result of this experience is that the person may be left with greater feelings of guilt and, thus, a greater degree of hesitancy to maintain conscious contact with God. Such an experience does not improve spirituality; it only contributes to a greater degree of isolation.

Second, a person can perceive the results of bargaining with God as "I carried out my part of the bargain, but God let me down." Such an experience often leaves a person skeptical, maybe even angry. The conclusion reached may be similar to Mark Twain's Huckleberry Finn:

> Miss Watson she took me in the closet and we prayed, but nothing came of it. She told me to pray every day, and whatever I asked for I would get it. But it warn't so. I tried it. I got a fishline, but no hooks. I tried for the hooks three or four times, but somehow I couldn't make it work. ...I set down one time back in the woods, and had a long think about it. I says to myself, if a body can get anything they pray for, why don't Deacon Winn get back the money he lost on pork? Why can't the widow get back her silver snuff box that was stole? Why can't Miss Watson fat up? No, says I to myself, there ain't nothing to it.

Such approaches to God usually result in greater alienation.

Third, a person may conclude that "God did His part, I did mine, and everything worked out." One would think that this would always be a positive experience -- and sometimes it is. However, out of this experience a person may conclude that he can "use" God to get the things he wants. Thus, he may begin to perceive God as similar to a cosmic slot machine into which he puts a prayer and takes out a blessing.

These three responses have one thing in common: *The person is trying to control God to achieve his own goals, rather than turning his will and his life over to the care of God.*

The third step prayer catches the essence of what we should do:

> God, I offer myself to Thee--to build with me and to do with me as you will. Relieve me of the bondage of self, that I may better do Thy will. Take away my difficulties, that victory over them may bear witness to those I would help by Thy power, Thy love, and Thy way of life. May I do Thy will always. Amen.

Our basic need is to surrender to God; to be ready to do His will.

Prayer as Talking to God. —Sometimes a person gets stymied in praying, thinking that prayers must be offered in a specific way. The following guidelines may be helpful as you pray.

First, use everyday language. Don't focus so much on "praying" as on just talking to God. Use conversational language, just as you might use with a person whom you respect.

Second, talk about your feelings. So frequently, people in addiction are out of touch with their feelings. We must be honest or prayer is useless. If in anger or bitterness, self-pity or despair, or selfish desire for things that are really unnecessary or in our human longing for deliverance from trouble or pain — if this is where we are, then this is where we must begin praying. To report one's feelings to God helps the person to get in touch with them.

Prayer, however, is more than just a human experience of getting in touch with our feelings; there is a God who hears and intervenes in His own time and in His own way.

Third, find your best point for communicating with God. Kneeling to pray is a physical act that expresses humility, but that is not the only way a person can pray. You may wish to try some creative ways to communicate with God. For example, write a prayer and read it aloud to God. Take a walk and talk out loud to God. Sit quietly and send your thoughts upward to God. Think a quick prayer when you face a difficult situation. These and other ways are all worthwhile efforts at praying. The main point is to make conscious contact with God and to live in a positive relationship with Him.

Prayer as Listening to God. — Prayer is not only talking with God; it is also listening to God, seeking to discover what he is communicating to us. When we refer to listening to God, we are not referring to hearing audible voices. Rather, we are referring to learning to understand and hear the ways God has spoken in days past and how he continues to speak to us today. Obviously, God can speak in any way He wishes; He is God. However, there are ways He speaks that can be specifically identified.

God speaks to us through nature. In the book of Psalms, it is written, "The heavens declare the glory of God." Many people find that they can feel closer to God when they are close to His natural world.

A patient at Cumberland Heights wrote of her experience.

> I've watched the sunrise at the pond today. I've seen God in all His wonder and majesty--the birds singing, water bugs skimming the surface like synchronized swimmers, fish jumping, crickets chirping. The trees ... the grass ... the wildflowers. The steam swirling off the pond as it rises, dancing as the breeze changes. The sun shining like a spotlight through the trees as it arose , announcing its arrival with a pink glow in the blue sky. As the sun crept closer into view, I was struck by the awe of the entire scene. No man or woman was responsible for the sunrise today, it just happened. No one told the birds to sing, it just happened. No human hand played a role in this early morning art--yet it all happened just as it was supposed to and does with great consistency each day. God has created a world of splendor for each of us. All we have to do is show up and be open to its beauty.

God speaks to us through circumstances and events that we encounter in life. That is what the Bible is — a record of how God revealed Himself through His mighty acts. God gave people the ability to perceive in these acts the messages that he was communicating. The writers recorded the messages that he was communicating. The writers recorded the messages for posterity. God gives those who are willing to see the ability to do so. Thus, circumstances become sanctuaries where we meet God.

God speaks to us through people. Throughout history, God has raised up people to carry his message. In the Old Testament, the prophets filled this role. Jesus and the Apostles filled this role in the New Testament. God still chooses people to communicate His message. God may appear in some of the most unusual places and in some of the most unusual ways. He may get inside a friend and use that friend to give us a message. That friend may not even be aware of it, because the emphasis is not on the person, but on the message. When the message is delivered, the person goes his way, but the message remains.

God speaks to us through direct revelation. He may give us new insights. Such revelations are always consistent with God's nature and the message God has shared in days past. Thus, one would do well to confirm his under-standing of such revelation by studying the Bible and by communicating with other persons in the community of faith.

From Alienation to Conscious Contact

Most of us agree that prayer is a good thing to do; fewer of us do it regularly. Regular prayer requires dis-cipline.

- Set a definite time for prayer. Begin each day with a prayer for God's help. Close the day with a prayer of thanksgiving. Pray during the day as you feel the need or desire. If you miss a time, don't despair. Simply get back on schedule.

- Look back over the pages of this chapter and underline the specific guidelines that you can implement as you pray each day.

Spirituality, one's relationship with the God of his under-standing, is fostered through communication. If we maintain conscious contact with God, the process of spirituality will work. It will affect all that we think and do.

---

*I have to live with myself, and so
I want to be fit for myself to know.
I don't want to pause at the set of the sun,
And hate myself for the things I have done.*

—*Edgar A. Guest*

The one regret I have is that I'm not someone else.

—*Woody Allen*

3

From
Self-Depreciation
to
Self-Esteem

One of the distinguishing marks of humankind is that since the dawn of creation we have been a problem for ourselves. In the words of David McCord, "Life is the garment we continuously alter, which never seems to fit."

One way we can be distinguished from the lower animals is that we have more needs than they do. Attempts to meet those needs have taken various avenues of expression.

Search for Survival

The quest for survival has frequently been identified as our greatest need. Certainly, there is some validity to this assertion. The need for self-preservation is strong, but people sometimes risk survival to reach goals they consider to be more precious than life itself. History is filled with records of many sensible people who have chosen to die in dignity rather than to live in shame.

Pursuit of Pleasure

Sigmund Freud advocated that the experience of pleasure was the primary motive for our actions. But what about that countless number of people who forsake pleasure in favor of duty? The desire of the eye, the stomach, the ear, and the body can be satisfied, leaving us with the plaguing question: "Is that all there is to life?"

Push for Power

Alfred Adler advocated that all of man's activities could be explained as the will to power. The indicting pages of history give evidence that we will kill our enemies, betray our friends, and even deceive ourselves in our push for power. But there is also ample evidence that once we achieve power, we are still not satisfied.

Frequently, power is misused as we search for something to give life greater meaning. In the 12 step program, recovery does not come from the push of power; rather it begins when a person admits and surrenders to his powerlessness. Because the addicted person's world is falling apart, he tries harder and harder to control it and put it back in order. Because of his addiction, his efforts are to little or no avail. That is why it is necessary to surrender — to admit that he is powerless over his addiction; that his life has become unmanageable. In so doing, he becomes ready to rely on a Power greater than himself.

Mandate for Meaning

During World War II, Victor Frankl experienced the injustices and pains of Nazi concentration camps. He was one of the minority of Jews who survived the devastating death blows of Nazi persecution. Out of his experience he wrote *Man's Search for Meaning* in which he advocated that the ability of a person to find meaning in life was his primary motivational force. "If I know why," Frankl asserted, "I can survive any how." Lack of meaning can result in a benign, mundane existence. However, the pursuit of meaning, per se, is like chasing a butterfly. The more you chase it, the more it eludes you. Meaning comes when a person is satisfied with himself.

Dream of Esteem

Our primary need is to experience self-esteem — to be "at home" with ourselves. Lack of self-esteem can prompt us to not want to survive. In fact, the majority of suicides are addiction related, which indicates that the addicted person has experienced erosion of self-esteem. Lack of self-esteem causes pleasure to escape us. Life becomes meaningless.

Regardless of whatever else addiction does, it robs a person of self-esteem.

Regardless of what ever else addiction does, it robs a person of self-esteem. The wall of feelings that separate us from God and others also separates us from our better selves. A vicious cycle develops in addiction. A person uses mood-altering chemicals in an effort to feel better, then feels worse because of the effects of his use. A downward spiral begins, resulting in a person feeling worse and worse about himself and feeling the need to use more and more mood-altering chemicals.

We all experience feelings that, if not dealt with appropriately, diminish self-esteem. Addicted persons seem to experience these feelings more dramatically and to a greater degree. In the following chapters, we will explore some of these feelings and how we may deal with them more appropriately. Certainly, medicating these feelings with mood-altering chemicals is not an appropriate way to deal with them. At times, we get temporary relief, but we do not deal constructively with the feelings. When we bury our feelings with mood-altering chemicals, we do not bury them dead; rather, we bury them alive and they continue to exist inside us, gnawing away at our self-esteem.

When we bury our feelings with mood altering chemicals, we do not bury them dead; rather, we bury them alive and they continue to exist inside us, gnawing away at our self-esteem.

The Esteem Triangle

Self-esteem is not achieved in isolation. It is inseparately related to how we experience other people. To a great extent, we are products of people who have loved us or failed to love us. It works like this. When other people affirm us, we tend to continue to do the things that have been affirmed. When they do not affirm us, our self-esteem begins to diminish. In addiction, the victim becomes isolated from other people. His primary relationship is with mood-altering chemicals. Thus, he becomes lonely and fails to experience positive reinforcement from other people and his self-esteem diminishes.

Self-esteem is also inseparably related to how we perceive and experience God. If we view God as a cruel or judgmental tyrant, as addicted persons frequently do, we will have difficulty believing that He loves us. Often, in addiction a person will attribute to God the characteristics of cruelty and judgment. Invariably, this concept of God is associated with feelings of low self-esteem. On the other hand, if we view God as a God of love, who is ready and willing to help us, our self-esteem is improved. Step 2 indicates not that we just believe in God, but that God will help us, that He is for us.

The esteem triangle is summarized in the biblical commandment: Love God and your neighbor as yourself. The three are an intricate web that holds our self-esteem together.

From Self-Depreciation to Self-Esteem

We live our way into patterns of thinking and feeling more frequently than we think or feel our way into patterns of living. If we wish to maintain healthy self-esteem, we must act in ways that allow us to feel worthwhile.

- Accept the fact that you are a unique person. When God created you, he made you unique from all other persons. He does not expect you to be like someone else; he expects you to be yourself and to be obedient to Him.

- Accept the fact that God loves you unconditionally. You do not have to earn his love; it is a grace gift. Accept the gift and cherish it. Knowing that God loves you will give you greater permission to begin to love yourself appropriately (see ch. 14).

- Seek the solace, comfort, and support of people who are willing to love you. Accept the love they offer. In addiction, a person tends to become isolated from other people. No wonder self-esteem diminishes. The person is left with no reinforcement; only his self-defeating addictive logic and feelings.

- When taking personal inventory (Step 4), recognize and accept the good as well as the bad. The future depends not only on getting rid of our character defects, but also on maximizing our strengths.

- Show genuine interest and concern for others. Self-esteem is enhanced when you treat others with esteem. It is multiplied as other people respond to you as a person of worth.

● Try to be more accepting of yourself. Each day, think of what you did right, and look on your mistakes as learning experiences.

● Keep a healthy balance between work and social life. Be careful not to spend too much time and energy in work. Instead, balance your life with loved ones, work, hobbies, and a group of friends or co-workers who respect you. In other words, seek positive reinforcement for your self-worth.

● Match dreams with reality. Are your goals realistic? If not, failure to achieve them may contribute to self-depreciation. Set reasonable goals and reward yourself when you achieve them.

● Identify your feelings and share them with a support group. Thus, you may receive guidance on how to deal with how you feel.

Before a person can be who he is and not pretend to be someone else, he must like who he is. One of the benefits of the 12 step program is that it helps a person to be that self which he truly is.

Half the harm done in the world is due to the people who want to feel important.

—T.S. Eliot

4
From
Grandiosity
to
Humility

In *The Spirit of Saint Louis,* Charles Lindbergh tells about his history-making flight to Paris. The secret of his success, he said, was in maintaining the proper altitude. If he flew too high, cold temperature might cause the wings of his plane to ice up. If he flew too low, a sudden dip of the plane might send him splashing into the ocean.[1] One's self-concept may be compared to that flight. While we should not continuously depreciate ourselves, neither should we harbor and nurture feelings of grandiosity.

Grandiosity is the feeling that we have the special privilege of being different from others. We want to do things our way, despite negative consequences. Grandiosity demands instant gratification of wishes and desires. It

37

frequently claims that there is nothing that cannot be mastered, even when all the facts indicate otherwise. We want what we want when we want it and we become frustrated if we don't get it. Such an attitude has little or no room for spirituality, because spirituality demands that we surrender our inflated ego and become willing to learn.

Grandiosity as Idolatry

Grandiosity is a form of idolatry. It is placing oneself in the place of God as the supreme authority in life. The first humans, Adam and Eve, did this. God told them not to eat of the tree of the knowledge of good and evil. They disregarded God's command and ate of the tree because they desired to be as wise as God. In other words, they sought to replace God with their own independence. Their relationship with God was up side down. Instead of acknowledging the sovereignty of God, they wanted to relegate God to a lesser role so they could be sovereign. They did so to their own demise — and we do too!

The story of Adam and Eve is not just a story of primeval humankind in a remote garden. It is the story of each of us.

The story of Adam and Eve is not just a story of primeval humankind in a remote garden. It is the story of each of us. We also are tempted and choose to be independent of God. But, like Adam and Eve, we do it to our own detriment. The truth is, we simply are not smart enough to run our own lives. We play havoc when we try.

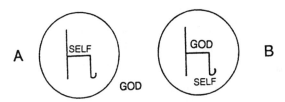

Diagram A illustrates how the grandiose person sees God. Diagram B illustrates how God is positioned in one's life as a result of Step 3:

> Made a decision to turn our wills and our lives over to the care of God, as we understand him.

Grandiosity as Isolation

Grandiosity leads a person to isolate himself from the presence and resources of others. In the same way he convinces himself that he does not need God, he also convinces himself that he does not need other people. Thus, he cuts himself off from other people - one of the primary mediums of God's grace. He does not listen to the counsel of others and is left to his own inadequate resources as he makes decisions about his behavior and actions. In fact, the grandiose person becomes frustrated and sometimes aggressive when his "superior" knowledge and ability are challenged or questioned. It is easy to see how such a person is "an alcoholic or an addict waiting to happen" long before he begins to drink or use.

Grandiosity as Self-Destructive Behavior

The Bible states that "Pride goes before a fall and a haughty spirit before destruction" (Prov. 16:18). Grandiosity leads to bad decision-making. Grandiosity leads a person to deny his problem and seek to justify his behavior. Because of grandiosity, a person will continue on a path that leads to self-destruction, unwilling to hear the counsel of others or consider the will of God. Inevitably, the consequences of such behavior are destructive. While grandiosity fuels addictive disorders, it is not limited to them. Grandiosity seems to be a human problem, not just an addiction problem. However, in addiction, the problem seems to magnify.

Grandiosity as Self-Deceit

Grandiosity is self-defeating because it is self-deceiving. In essence, the grandiose person is out of touch with reality. He or she is trying to become convinced that they are self-sufficient, but, in reality, it is the "self-sufficiency that is not sufficient."

Grandiosity is often a camouflage for fear.

Grandiose behavior is often a camouflage for fear. The grandiose person is like a little boy walking through a cemetery at night, telling himself that he is not scared. He really is scared; he just won't admit it, and the more afraid he becomes, the faster he walks and the louder he whistles.

From Grandiosity to Humility

If grandiosity is the supreme character defect—and leading theologians for centuries have so stated—it follows that humility, its opposite, is a primary virtue.

Humility is dependence on God and others, while grandiosity is an attempt to be self-sufficient.

Humility makes us receptive to God's grace; grandiosity alienates us from God and spurns God's grace when it is offered.

Humility is openness to learn; grandiosity is closed mindedness. Minds are like parachutes; they function properly only if they are open.

Humility leads to identification with other people; grandiosity leads to isolation from other people.

Humility is cooperative; grandiosity is competitive.

Obviously, humility is preferred over grandiosity. How can we cultivate this virtue in our lives so we may practice spirituality in a more conscious manner?

- Learn from the experiences of suffering. That statement is made with the assumption that grandiosity will inevitably lead to pain and suffering in our lives. While suffering is not something we should seek, it does teach us an important fact of life: We are not entirely self-sufficient. Thus, suffering can be a "teacher" that helps us to learn humility.

- Remember that we have nothing that we have not received as a gift. God, in his grace, has provided all the resources we have. Thus, giving God credit rather than taking credit ourselves can help us to maintain an attitude of humility.

- Remember that we are utterly dependent on the mercy and grace of God for whatever we hope to achieve in life, whether it be material goods, internal happiness, or rewarding relationships.

- Be courteous toward other people. Remember that each of us is created in the image of God and, therefore, deserve respect.

- Turn loose of the idea that you must always be right; that you are smarter than other people. That may or may not be true, but it really doesn't matter.

- Give other people credit freely, even at your own expense, believing that the credit you gave away will return to you as other people give you credit.

- Credit given by others is much preferred over credit that you claim for yourself.

- Be cautious about practices that are related to showing off or bragging. Probably, it would be best to do things for others in privacy.

- Make amends as often as necessary, even when the other person is partly to blame for the trouble. Sweep your own side of the street, even if others leave theirs cluttered.

A Zen proverb states, "When the mind is ready, a teacher will appear." In the same manner, when the heart is ready, God will appear. Humility is a prerequisite for God's presence to work in and through our lives.

Notes

1. Charles A. Lindbergh, *The Spirit of Saint Louis* (New York: Scribner's, 1953), ch. 6.

Forgiving yourself means giving up hope for a better past.

—*John A. MacDougall*

5

From
Guilt
to
Forgiveness

Tracy had spent more than two hours in the office sharing her fifth step. The counselor listened to what she said but also to what she implied, the undercurrent feelings of her words. Over and over the counselor sensed her feeling of alienation from God and her low self-esteem. Finally, she told the "big" thing that had bothered her for years. At age 18, Tracy had an abortion. She did not tell her family. They were strict Irish Catholics and she felt certain they would not accept her action. The only other people who knew about the abortion were the man with whom she had sexual relations and the medical personnel who performed the abortion. But Tracy was keenly aware that another person knew about it. God knew about it—and this caused deep pain of guilt that she had lived with for 10 years.

Step 5 reads:

> We admitted to God, to ourselves, and to another human being the exact nature of our wrongs.

Thereby is the beginning of healing for guilt.

Guilt is the distressing feeling a person experiences when he has violated his own code of conduct. The distressing feeling contributes to low self-esteem and, for people who are inclined to medicate their feelings, to use mood-altering chemicals in an effort to feel better.

Guilt as an Over-Active Conscience

Sometimes people experience guilt because of an over-active conscience. Such people may feel guilty when there is no apparent reason for doing so. "Let your conscience be your guide" is a common cliche, but it is not a very good rule to live by. *Conscience does not tell us what is right or wrong; it tells us whether we have acted according to what we believe to be right or wrong.* Conscience is the rules that we have internalized into our value system. The person who has no internalized rules has problems with appropriate behavior. However, the person who is excessively rule-bound tends to be inflexible in his thinking and behavior. He sets rigid standards for himself and feels guilty when he fails to achieve them.

An overactive, accusative conscience is often the result of the teachings of authority figures in our past. The fear of punishment and the desire for love and acceptance prompt us to try to keep the rules imposed by these authority figures. If the rules are too demanding, we may either rebel or become guilt-ridden. The person who becomes guilt-ridden in this fashion may feel guilt for no apparent reason.

Customs that were expedient for one generation sometimes become "ethical" for the next. A graphic illustration of this is provided by Thomas Harris in his book *I'm OK, You're OK.* He told the story of a lady who always cut off both the hock and the butt of a ham before she placed it in the oven to cook. When asked by her husband why she did it, she defended her actions by saying, "That's how mother always did it." A few weeks later when visiting her mother, she asked, "Why did you cut off both ends of the ham?" In her reply, the mother explained that the ham was prepared that way because the oven was too small to accommodate a full-sized ham. A lot of our "oughts" are like that. They have no inherent ethical value — we simply continue to do them because that is how they are "supposed" to be done. Such customs deserve to be examined to determine if they are worthy of preservation. If they are not, they should be discarded without feelings of guilt.

The excessively rule-bound person has difficulty accepting his humanity.

The excessively rule-bound person has difficulty accepting his humanity. His perfectionistic attitude causes him to over-expect from himself and others. Like the prince of Tyrus, of whom Ezekiel wrote, he needs to be reminded "that you are a man and not God, though you set your heart as the heart of God" (Ezek. 28:2).

Guilt as Trespasses Against Others

While guilt may result from a conscience wound too tight, obviously, this is not the only origin. *Anyone who feels severely guilty is usually blaming himself for something quite specific. In other words, he knows he has something to feel guilty about.*

Often feelings of guilt come from the way we have treated other people. We have trespassed against them, and these trespasses are the source of our guilt. Later in this chapter we will discuss how making amends to people we have harmed contributes to our ability to forgive ourselves for what we have done.

Guilt as Transgression Against God

God is always involved in our guilt, whether it results from an over-active conscience, trespasses against others, or a transgression of God's will. One of the reasons for guilt is that God will not leave us alone in our transgression. If he did, we probably would continue our transgression to our own demise. Out of his grace, He pricks us with feelings of guilt. In this sense, guilt is one expression of God's love. God does not cause the guilt, but He can use it in a redemptive way.

Guilt Games We Play

Guilt is such a painful feeling that it cannot be ignored. It demands attention. One way people sometimes deal with their guilt is through *denial.* In other words, they try to convince themselves that there is nothing to feel guilty about when in fact there is. This approach is self deceiving. No relief is found, because deep inside one knows the truth.

Another way often used to deal with guilt is *minimization,* in which a person tries to discount the severity of the problem. "I may have done wrong," they say, "but my behavior is not as bad as some other people." This approach may provide some temporary "false" relief, but it does not deal with the heart of the problem.

Attempts at *justification* of one's behavior is another way that people try to deal with guilt. Dishonest thinking is used as a means of trying to calm the storm of guilt that blows within.

Perfectionism is yet another attempt to deal with guilt. The person seeks to earn his right to be forgiven. The futility of this approach is that while the person tries to earn his right to be forgiven, he continues to do things that add to his guilt, thus, becoming more and more frustrated.

Some people deal with their guilt by "psychologizing it." Through *rationalization* they seek to deal with their guilt feelings. Like the man described by David Head in his book, *He Sent Leanness,* they pray, "We confess that we have lost all our ideals, but congratulate ourselves that we have reached that stage of maturity which makes it possible to live without such adolescent encumbrances."[1]

When we fail to deal appropriately with guilt, we tend to bury it within us. Then we become the victims of unconscious guilt — guilt of which we are not consciously aware. Unconscious guilt may lead us to seek retribution through self-punishment. In other words, we take our wrongs upon ourselves, rather than confessing them to God and claiming forgiveness.

Guilt can lead not only to self-punishment, but also to projection of guilt upon others. The person who is continuously hypercritical of other people may well ask, "Am I acting out unconscious feelings of guilt--guilt that I need to admit and deal with."

The authentic way to deal with guilt is through experiencing forgiveness.

The authentic way to deal with guilt is to experience forgiveness. The first step is to experience the forgiveness of God. Such forgiveness is offered as a gift of grace.

If forgiveness is a grace gift, how do we receive it? It is there for the asking. First, we must *acknowledge* our need for forgiveness rather than deny it. The next step is to *admit* the wrongs that need to be forgiven. When we are willing to admit our need for forgiveness, we place ourselves in the position to receive the forgiveness that is offered. It will not come from denial, minimizing, justifying, working for it or rationalizing it. Forgiveness comes only as a gift, which we in humility and gratitude become willing to receive. Thus, the final step is to *accept* the forgiveness that is offered – to believe that God has forgiven us.

When we experience the forgiveness of God, we are led to forgive others (see ch. 7 on resentments) and seek the forgiveness of others. Because we have received the forgiveness of God, we desire to live in right relationship with others. Thoughts of how we have harmed others may continue to plague us until we attempt to set things right with them.

While making amends should not be an attempt to earn God forgiveness, it does help us to forgive ourselves. Self-forgiveness is often more difficult to experience than the forgiveness of God. Often it is a process that requires continued effort. Ultimately, self-forgiveness will come as we realize that we have been forgiven by God.

From Guilt to Forgiveness

Forgiveness is more than a concept; it is an experience. The following activities can help you achieve this experience.

- Own your feelings of guilt. When you deny, rationalize, minimize, or justify your guilt, it continues to erode your self-esteem.

- Talk to God about your guilt—both the feeling and the actions that led to the feeling. Ask for forgiveness. Claim the promise of forgiveness to those who sincerely ask.

- Follow the 12 step program as you work on forgiving yourself. God's forgiveness is an event - it happens at the time a person asks for forgiveness. Forgiving yourself is a process—and that process is often more difficult to experience than the event of God's forgiveness. We know that God is good and merciful, but we believe that we are not. Thus, it may be impossible to forgive yourself by yourself; you may need the power of God to accomplish this. Steps 1, 2, and 3 may be adapted to ask God to help us to forgive ourselves. For example:

(1) We admitted we were powerless over our inability to forgive ourselves; that it was unmanageable.

(2) Came to believe that God, who has forgiven us, could help us to forgive ourselves.

(3) Made a decision to turn over to the care of God our inability to forgive ourselves. In so doing, we ask God to move in our lives and our circumstances to do for us what we cannot do for ourselves.

- Another way to experience forgiveness of self is to make amends to persons we have harmed. No amount of self-depreciation can ease the pain of our guilt or remedy our wrongs. The man who has neglected his family may tell himself that he is no good, but that will not meet his family's needs. The woman who feels that she has neglected her children will not help her children by punishing herself with guilt. The challenge is to move away from our guilt through self-forgiveness and, insofar as reasonably possible, make amends for the harm that has been done. To the extent we can do this, to that extent we will feel better about ourselves.

- Be aware that there are some things, however, for which we cannot make amends. Some actions are like water poured from a bucket into the sand. It is impossible to return the water to the bucket.

Some of the damages we have done are like that. In such cases, we can place those persons into the grace of God. The same God of grace who is willing to forgive us is also willing to work in the lives of persons we have harmed to bring about healing.

There is a positive side of guilt. It indicates that an individual who feels it is not a hopeless person. Hopeless people don't feel guilty; they are incapable of it. Thus, guilt contains an element of hope. The hope is actualized in feeling the need for forgiveness and experiencing it.

Notes

1. David Head, *He Sent Leanness* (New York:The MacMillan Company), 1962, p. 20

Love anything and your heart will be wrung and possibly broken. If you want to make sure of keeping it intact you must give it to no one, not even an animal. Wrap it carefully round you with hobbies and little luxuries; avoid all entanglements. Lock it up safe in the casket or coffin of your selfishness. But in that casket—safe, dark, motionless, airless—it will change. It will not be broken; it will become unbreakable, impenetrable, irredeemable.

To love is to be vulnerable.

—C.S. Lewis

I know God has promised that he will not place on me more than I can bear, but sometimes I wish He didn't trust me so much.

—Mother Teresa

6

From
Grief
to
Acceptance

He had been dead for five years when Sharon entered treatment, but she had never said good-bye. She and Bill had a good marriage. She spoke of the good times. Travel together — mutual friends, couples like them. Now Bill was dead. It came suddenly — a heart attack that was so massive he had no chance to recover. Bill did not linger long. One day he appeared to be in good health, the next day he was dead.

Sharon felt the hurt deeply. She remembered that she and Bill would sometimes take a drink or two with a meal. She remembered how it made her feel better. She needed something to make her feel better now, so she decided to have a few drinks. At first, she had only a few. Then they increased to more than she ever had before. Soon she drank every day—not a little, but a lot. It killed the pain that was deep in her heart.

As her drinking continued, she discovered that the drinking itself was causing pain, but she could not seem to stop. Attempts to medicate her feelings of grief had led to addiction.

In many cases, trauma and the accompanying grief lead to and fuel addictive behavior. Then the addictive behavior prevents a person from adequately moving through the grieving process.

Grief—A Universal Experience

If we live long enough, we will experience grief. We all lose things and persons whom we have come to love. Grief is the emotional response to the loss.

Grief can be experienced from any perceived loss.

Usually, we think of grief in terms of the loss of a loved one, but grief can be experienced from many other losses. For example, the loss of youth (getting old) can be an occasion for grief. Likewise, grief can occur from the loss of a relationship, such as in divorce. *Wherever there is perceived loss, there is grief.* Thus, grief can be slight or great, depending on our perception of the extent of the loss.

Grief not only occurs after a loss; the anticipation of a loss can be an occasion for grief. For example, one might begin to grieve for a loved one before the loved one dies. Usually, such grief is accompanied with anxiety as one realizes that the loss is imminent.

Stages of Grief

Grief is a process that moves through predictable stages. The first stage is *shock,* which is usually accompanied with an emotional numbness. The grieving person has very little feelings and may move through the actions necessitated by the loss with apparent "courage." We believe this numbness is often a manifestation of the grace of God — given to us to help deal with the responsibilities incurred by the loss.

The second stage of grief is *fantasy.* A person may unconsciously deny that the loss has occurred. For example, one wife who had lost her dearly loved husband admitted that each evening she would unconsciously begin to think about preparing the evening meal in anticipation of the arrival of her husband, then face the reality that he was dead and would not be coming to dinner.

The third stage of grief is the *realization* of what has happened and is usually accompanied by hostility or anger. The grieving person may direct the anger at self, feeling depressed that he or she has in some way failed to do all that should have been done to prevent the loss. The anger may be directed toward other persons, perhaps the doctor who attended the person who died or the boss for whom the person worked. At times, the anger may be directed toward the person who died. "He just died and left me," Sarah said, as she grieved the loss of Bill, her husband. The anger may be directed at God. "Why did you do this to me?", the person may ask God. When people ask God "why," they are not really asking for an explanation. If they are given an explanation, they will retort with an argument. Usually, when people ask why, they are really asking another question: "God, do you still love? Are you still there?"

The fourth stage of grief is *release,* which usually is accompanied by a "flood of grief." It is necessary, and thus important, to express our grief in order to move through it. In such cases, grieving is very healing—and the person should be allowed to grieve. They must walk through the valley of grieving before they can reach the mountain of hope that awaits on the other side.

The final stage of grief is *acceptance* of the loss and the restructuring of life around new goals and new meaning. The final stage cannot be reached until the person has moved through the previous stages.

The time needed for a person to move through the grief process varies with different persons and the extent of the impact of the loss. Usually, there is a "back and forth" motion in the various stages of grief. Normally, the process moves forward, even if it is slow at times.

In most cases, grief is the pain that heals itself. It is possible, however, to become "stymied" in the grief process, particularly in the anger stage. Thus, a person may remain angry at self, or depressed. Or, the person may remain angry at God, or rebellious. Or the person may remain angry at someone else, or resentful. These feelings—depression, rebellion, resentment—are obviously painful feelings. Persons inclined toward addiction may begin to medicate these feelings with mood-altering chemicals. The result is immediate and temporary relief. Having been rewarded with temporary relief, the person may repeat the behavior. If this cycle is carried out over an extended period of time, the person may become physically and psychologically addicted. All the while, the grief has been medicated, but continues to lie dormant within the person. In such cases, healing requires that the person own and express the grief. The floodgates of the emotions, which have been closed, must be opened to allow the grief to pour out. When this happens, healing begins to occur. The person can begin to move toward acceptance of the loss and to the restructuring of life.

STAGES OF GRIEF

Shock > Fantasy > Realization > Release > Acceptance

From Grief to Acceptance

How easy it is in times of grief to feel that God is not near. Such, however, is not the case. The Bible teaches, "Surely he has borne our grief...." (Isa. 53:4). We do well to remember that God walks with us through the valleys as well as on the mountain.

The grief process can become stymied, but it can seldom be hurried. A person needs time to grieve. There are, however, actions that a person can take to facilitate his moving through the process of grief. Also, there comes a time when a person must make a deliberate effort to move on with life.

- Face the fact of the loss. Denying it will prolong the grief. Even tell yourself out loud that you have lost the thing or person that is the source of your grief. If the source is a person, see the body, if possible. This will help you confront the reality and begin your grief work.

- Don't engage in self-torturing doubts about whether the loss could have been prevented. What's done is done.

- Let yourself feel all the feelings. The more you fully allow the feelings to come out, the sooner they will begin to fade and gradually disappear. Then you can begin to rebuild your life around new goals.

- If your grief is anticipatory (the loss has not happened, but it is imminent) share your feelings with someone. If a person is dying, share your feelings with that person. Express your love. Try to resolve unfinished business in your relationship. Such will minimize your regrets later.

- Accept the help of other people. Don't try to "be brave" and do everything by yourself. Isolation in such cases only prolongs the feelings of grief. If you attend a support group, increase the frequency of your attendance. Talk about how you feel. Be open to receive the love that other people offer.

- Take comfort in your spiritual commitments. Try

to understand that losing is as much a part of life as receiving. Above all, don't doubt the love of the God of your understanding. Take comfort in the hope that God has taken the person to be with Him, where his spirit exists in a perfect and happy state. Thank God for allowing the person to be a part of your life.

• Take time to sift through the memories and objects related to the loss. For example, if the loss is a person, do something constructive with the belongings left. If the loss is something other than a person, sift through them and decide what to keep and what to discard. This process will help you to move along in your grief work.

• Have a conversation in your mind with the dead person or the object of loss. To be more explicit, you may want to write a letter. Say all the things you wish you had said. And, most of all, say goodbye.

• Let go of the source of your grief and dedicate yourself to the future. Realize that even though you are letting go, you will always have the memory of your loss inside you.

• Fully accept the challenge to rebuild your life. When you have done your grieving well, you will have regained strength, wisdom, compassion and an appreciation of life. Make specific plans to move forward in life. Celebrate and be grateful for the aliveness you find in and around you.

We are sometimes called upon to walk through the

valley, but remember that we will walk through it and that God has promised to walk through it with us. "Surely he has borne our griefs and carried our sorrows..." (Isa. 53:4).

Resentment is the "number one" offender. It destroys more alcoholics than anything else. From it stem all forms of spiritual disease, for we have been not only mentally and physically ill, we have been spiritually sick.

—*Alcoholics Anonymous, p. 64*

7

From
Resentment
to
Understanding

Brian had responded very positively to the 12 step program. His fifth step was a very meaningful event. He told of the following story:

> When I was twelve years old, I was rummaging through the drawers of a dresser in my parents' bedroom when I found my birth certificate. I was puzzled because the last name on the certificate was different from the name I had been called for as long as I could remember—the same name as my parents. Secretly, I concluded that I must have been adopted and said nothing about my discovery. After all, I was not supposed to have been plundering in my parents' dresser drawer.

When I was 18, my parents told me the truth. My mother had divorced my father soon after I was born. Soon thereafter she married the man I had always thought was my father. Her name was changed by the marriage, but mine remained the same. Legally, I had the same name as my biological father, although I had never seen him.

My parents told me where my "real" father lived. A few days later, I boarded a plane and travelled to see him. He was at the airport when I arrived. As soon as I entered the terminal, I spotted him. I knew he was my father before we ever spoke to each other.

The man who was my "real" father had not communicated with me during my lifetime. Now he was opposed to my changing my name. He wanted me to retain his name, although I was of legal age to choose my last name without his consent.

In an effort to convince me to keep his name, he told how he had deposited $5,000 each year for the last 15 years into a bank account for me. "I'll give you that money now," he said, "if you will agree to keep my name."

His face flushed with anger as his mouth released a curse. With forceful anger he stated, "First, he abandoned me, then he wanted to buy my love. I returned home and took the name of the man who had raised me, the one who had been a real father to me."

The story did not end there, however. For 21 years, Brian's resentment toward his biological father had lived inside him. It was one of the primary factors that fueled his addiction.

While Brian's story is unique, resentment is not. All of us are confronted with it. The question is, How shall we handle it?

Resentment as Cold Anger

Anger is a common emotion experienced at various times by everyone. It is always a secondary emotion that expresses a feeling of hurt, fear, or frustration. It is a signal, just as is acute pain, that something is wrong and changes are necessary from within to restore balance or equilibrium. Anger is an internal signal of impending threat.

Anger can be "hot" or "cold." Hot anger is an explosive response to something that happens to us. Cold anger is a vengeful attitude buried within a person as a result of being hurt or frightened. Resentment looks for an opportunity to get even. It is like an iceberg; only a small portion of it may show, but the mass of it is beneath the surface. However, the fact that it is often obscure does not diminish its effect. Moreover, the addicted person tends to have more resentment because of his emotional pain. The pain causes resentment and the resentment fuels addictive behavior.

Resentment can be considered "re-sentiment." We continue to feel the feelings of anger long after the occasion that prompted them.

Resentment is re-sentiment; feeling the angry feelings over and over again.

67

Resentment as Loss of Control

When a person harbors and nurtures resentment toward another person, he loses control of his decision-making processes. He no longer acts freely; he reacts toward the person he resents. This reactive pattern means that the person who resents is not in control. Rather, the person who is resented is in control.

In *None of These Diseases,* the author states:

> I have found that the moment I start hating a man, I become his slave. I can't enjoy my work anymore because he even controls my thoughts. My resentments release excessive stress hormones and I become fatigued after only a few hours of work. The work I formerly enjoyed is now drudgery, and my brightly papered office seems like a dreary dungeon. Even vacations lose their pleasure. It may be a luxurious car that I drive along a lake fringed with the multi-colored autumnal beauty of maple, oak, and birch; but moping in my resentment, I might as well be driving a hearse in mud and rain.

> The man I hate hounds me wherever I go. I can't escape his tyrannical grasp on my mind. When the waiter serves me steamed lobster and clams, with asparagus, crisp salad, and strawberry shortcake smothered with ice cream, it might as well be stale bread and water. My teeth chew the food and I swallow it, but the man I hate will not allow me to enjoy it.

> The man I hate may be many miles from my bedroom; but more cruel than any slave driver, he whips my thoughts into such a frenzy that my 'perfect sleeper' mattress becomes a rack of torture. The lowliest of serfs can sleep, but not I. I am, indeed, a slave to every man I hate.[1]

If you cannot forgive people for their sake or for God's sake, do it for your own sake, so you can be free from resentment and able to choose the good life.

Resentment as Lack of Forgiveness

How frequently have you prayed the Lord's Prayer? If you are like most persons in a 12 step program, you have lost count. Look up this prayer in the Gospel of Matthew. It is located in Matthew 6: 9-13. Now continue to read verses 14-15, the verses that immediately follow the prayer. They read as follows:

For if you forgive men for their transgressions, your heavenly Father will also forgive you. But if you do not forgive men, then your Father will not forgive your transgressions (Matt. 6:14-15).

These verses state that if we want to experience God's forgiveness, we must forgive others. If we do not forgive, we cannot be forgiven. In other words, we cannot expect God to forgive us while we continue to harbor hate for another person. The two just do not mix.

The one who says he is in the light and yet hates his brother is in the darkness until now (1 John 2:9).

To be forgiven, we must forgive.

Resentment as Isolation

When we resent other people we tend to withdraw from them. In isolation we try to bury our feelings inside us. But the feelings gnaw at us, giving us emotional discomfort. Such uncomfortable feelings frequently fuel addiction. Moreover, isolation prevents us from resolving the issue for which we feel resentful, because we cut off communication. In isolation, the resentment tends to grow, rather than diminish.

From Resentment to Understanding

There seems to be no process through which one naturally moves to rid himself of resentment. Getting rid of it takes effort. Where does one begin?

- First, identify the persons toward whom you hold resentment. Usually, they are the persons who have caused you hurt or fear — maybe both.

- Second, realize that the resentment you hold is not someone else's problem; it is yours. Someone else may have done you an injustice, but the feelings you have about that person and the injustice are exclusively yours. You are responsible for that feeling.

- Third, indicate to God in prayer that you want to work on getting rid of your resentment and that you need his grace to help you do it.

- Fourth, ask God to help you to understand why these people hurt you. Remember that people do not just "do things," they do them for a reason. Often we do not know the reason. However, if we can understand the reason, we may find it easier to forgive the person who has harmed us. Keep in mind that behind anger is hurt, behind hurt is unmet expectation, and behind unmet expectation is unmet need. Was the person who harmed you simply trying to meet a need as they perceived it?

- Fifth, pray for the health, happiness and well-being of the persons you resent. Call the persons by name. Picture their faces in your mind. As you do this, you will be carrying out the biblical teachings of praying for your enemies. This is part of the process of being set free from resentment.

- Sixth, as soon as you have an opportunity, say something good about the persons you resent. They are not all bad; your perception of them is skewed because of your pain. Find some good traits they possess and tell someone about them.

- Seventh, when you have opportunity, do something good for these people. Don't do it for recognition; just do it. Even if you do not really want to do it, just do it!

The seven steps listed above can be repeated as often as necessary. Resentment sometimes dies a slow death. Like the proverbial cat, it can have nine lives. Keep on praying — as frequently and as many times as necessary — until the iceberg of resentment is melted away.

Notes

1. S. I. McMillen, *None of These Diseases* (Old Tappan, New Jersey: Fleming H. Revell, 1984), p. 116

*Nobody loves me; everybody hates me. I think I'll
go out in the garden and eat some worms.*

—Anonymous

Poor me. Pour me another drink.

—A practicing alcoholic

8

From
Self-Pity
to
Gratitude

Jerry "teared up" every time we talked. Life had not been easy for the past few months, but nothing devastating had happened. Still, he felt sorry for himself and that feeling was robbing him of his happiness and self-esteem. His self-pity also was the occasion for his continuing to drink alcohol and use other mood-altering chemicals.

Feelings of self-pity invade our lives at times. During such times, we may feel all alone and cut off from God. We may feel that God has deserted us. The question is, Shall we wallow in our feelings of self-pity or seek to deal with those feelings in a constructive manner?

Self-Pity as Unrealistic Expectations

Often we set ourselves up for feelings of self-pity because of unrealistic expectations. Then, when things don't work out as we expect, we feel sorry for ourselves. We expect life to be easier than it is. When it is not easy, we become disillusioned.

Scott Peck, in *The Road Less Travelled,* reminds us:

> Life is difficult. This is a great truth, one of the greatest truths. It is a great truth because once we see this truth, we transcend it. Once we truly know that life is difficult —once we truly understand and accept it—then life is no longer difficult. Because once it is accepted, the fact that life is difficult no longer matters. Most do not duly see this truth that life is difficult. Instead, they moan more or less incessantly, noisily or subtly, about the enormity of their problems, their burdens, and their difficulties as if life were generally easy, as if life should be easy. They voice their belief, noisily and subtly, that their difficulties represent a unique kind of affliction that should not be and that has somehow been especially visited upon them, or else upon their families, their tribe, their class, their nation, their race or even their species, and not upon others. I know about this moaning because I have done my share. Life is a series of problems. Do we want to moan about them or solve them?[1]

It is reasonable to expect that we will have problems; it is unreasonable to expect that we can live life without them. The issue is not whether or not we have problems, rather, it is how we deal with them.

74

Oh, a trouble's a ton, or a trouble's an ounce.
Or trouble is what you make it
And it isn't the fact that you're hurt that counts,
But only how did you take it?[2]

Self-Pity as Skewed Perception

Another reason for self-pity is skewed perception of reality. We may develop a mind set that encourages us to see only the negative things that are happening to us to the exclusion of the positive. With this mind set, we may begin to question God's goodness, not because His goodness is not manifested, but because we are not in a spiritual posture to see it.

Self-pity creates a sense of urgency, discomfort that causes people to seek relief. Frequently, the relief is sought through the use of alcohol or pills. Such relief, if it comes at all, is temporary. Since most mood-altering chemicals are depressants, rather than stimulants, they usually contribute to feelings of self-pity, rather than helping the person to overcome them.

From Self-Pity to Gratitude

The most effective antidote for self-pity is gratitude. It is virtually impossible to have self-pity and gratitude at the same time.

Gratitude is not circumstantial; it is attitudinal.

Gratitude is not circumstantial; rather it is attitudinal. Gratitude is internal — a way of looking at the world. Some people hold to the notion that gratitude is the result of external events. If something good happens, they feel grateful. If something bad happens, they are ungrateful and sad. But life does not bear out such expectations. Some people seem to have everything but gratitude itself. Other people seem to lack a lot of things but express an abundance of gratitude which leads to feelings of happiness.

When you sense feelings of self-pity arising within you, try the following things:

- Make a list of things for which you can be truly grateful. Counting your blessings is still a good thing to do, if you start from an attitude of gratitude. Lay that list before you and present it to God in prayer. Thank him for the good things you are experiencing. Place into his care the things that are unmanageable in your life. If this does nothing else — and it probably will do a lot more — it will help you to place the negatives and the positives of your life into proper perspective.

- Share with other people the things for which you are grateful. Do this humbly, lest someone interpret it as expressions of grandiosity.

- Don't allow other people to pity you. Empathy is affirming; pity is demeaning. If you accept the pity of others, it can only contribute to your feelings of self-pity.

- Don't assume that all the negative things that you are experiencing are necessarily bad. God, who can take a crucifixion and make a resurrection out of it, can take our unfortunate experiences and turn them into blessings. If you will reflect on your past, whatever virtues you possess probably came not from the good things that happened to you, but from the painful experiences that made you more open to learn. C. S. Lewis reminds us that God whispers to us in our pleasures, but he shouts to us in our pain.

- View your problems as opportunities, rather than discouragements. Leslie Weatherhead, one of England's great spiritual leaders, said: "I can only write down this simple testimony. Like all men, I prefer the sunny uplands of experience when health, happiness, and success abound; but I have learned more about God, life, and myself in the darkness ... than I ever learned in the sunshine.... The darkness, thank God, passes, but what one learns in the darkness he possesses forever."

The Bible is filled with admonitions about being thankful or grateful. These teachings are not there just because they are nice things to do. They are there to help us to achieve the abundant life that God offers.

Notes

1. Scott Peck, *The Road Less Travelled* (New York: Simon and Schuster, 1978), p. 15.

2. Edmund Vance Cook, "How Did You Die," taken from *Masterpieces of Religious Verse* (New York: Harper Brothers, 1948), p. 377.

Don't worry about things—food, drink, clothes. For you already have life and a body—and they are far more important than what to eat or wear. Look at the birds! They don't worry about what to eat—they don't need to sow or reap or store up food—for your heavenly Father feeds them. And you are far more valuable to him than they are. Will all your worries add a single moment to your life?

So don't be anxious about tomorrow, God will take care of your tomorrow too. Live one day at a time.

—The Living Bible, Matthew 6:25-27, 34

9

From
Anxiety
to
Security

One man walked up to another and asked directions to a hotel. No response. He asked again. No response, not even the turn of the head. The first man, irritated at being ignored, said, "Listen, buddy, I asked you a civil question. If you do not know how to get to that hotel, you could say so. You could at least be respectful."

Then the second man turned his head, looked the first fellow over head to toe, and said, "So you want to know how to get to the hotel? I'll give you directions and you will say 'thank you' and I'll say, 'Quite alright'; you will say, 'Nice day, isn't it?' Then I'll say, 'Yes, it is.' You will say, 'Who do you think will win the ball game this afternoon?'

I'll say, 'Not sure; what do you think.' And you'll say, 'By the way, my name is Tom Brown.' I'll say, 'Glad to know you, Tom; mine's Jim Smith. Why don't we have a cup of coffee together.' You'll say, 'Fine, let's do.' Over the cup of coffee I will invite you to my house. I have a daughter. You will meet my daughter, fall in love with her, marry her and have a house full of kids. Then you'll get sick and die and leave those kids for me to take care of. I don't like kids. No, I'm not going to tell you how to get to that hotel."

This story, humorous though it may be, illustrates what anxiety is all about. It is the fear that we cannot cope with past, present, or future events or circumstances. It is a threatening feeling for which the source is sometimes difficult to identify.

Anxiety is a threatening feeling for which the source is sometimes difficult to identify.

Anxiety and fear are very similar, the main difference being that fear is usually attached to a specific object outside the person and anxiety is a threatening or apprehensive feeling within the person that may have no specific external object to which it can be attached. It is conditioned by past experiences, experienced in the present, and projected into the future.

Sources of Anxiety

Anxiety has many sources. One source is what insurance companies call pre-existing conditions — *unpleasant experiences from the past,* maybe even childhood experiences that we do not consciously remember. Because they were unpleasant, we may have unconsciously buried them. In addition, some anxious feelings come from things we remember quite well, things that were unpleasant that we fear may happen again.

As you grow in your 12 step program, you will have an opportunity to explore your family of origin. Such exploration probably should not be done in detail until you have been active in the program six months to a year, because other issues, namely, your immediate sobriety, should have precedence. However, the time will come when you will want and need to explore family of origin issues as a process of continuing recovery. As you do this, you will gain greater insight into why you feel anxious about certain things.

Another source of anxiety is *present circumstances* — stressful conditions over which we feel powerless. How can I pay that bill which is overdue? What will people think when they find out about me? What if I have a dreaded, even fatal disease? All of us have at least some anxieties that arise from the stressful circumstances of life.

Anxieties exist to a greater degree among addicted persons.

Such anxieties may be assumed to exist in greater portions when a person is victimized by addiction to a mood-altering chemical. Use of the mood-altering chemical increasingly becomes the central interest in the person's life. As use increases, neglect of daily responsibilities occurs. "Left to themselves, things go from bad to worse," is one of Murphy's Laws. The addicted person's world begins to fall apart. Such deterioration may be manifested in health, finances, vocation, and/or family relationships. Frequently, as problems mount, so does one's use, resulting in the problems of life getting worse.

Finally, our anxiety comes from *projecting into the future.* No one has a crystal ball to see the future. And that probably is a good thing. We are admonished both in scripture and the 12 step program to live one day at a time.

Worry or anxiety seems to be the way we deal with the future if we seek to deal with it alone, without the help and care of God. But we are absolutely powerless over most of the unpredicted happenings of the future. That over which we are powerless is dealt with spiritually in Steps 2 and 3. We come to believe that the God who has been with us in the past and is with us in the present will also be with us in the future. We do not know what the future holds, but we know who holds the future – a gracious God who will be with us in all the circumstances of life, sharing our joys and our sorrows.

Some anxieties are a normal part of life.

Let us hasten to add that some anxiety is normal and, in fact, sometimes helpful. In a crisis, normal anxiety will allow one to anticipate and sometimes avoid possible disaster. Such anxiety is usually temporary, leaving us as the crisis subsides. Prolonged anxiety, however, sets one up for a constant state of needless worry. Projection takes over and all one can anticipate then is negative. In *Alcoholics Anonymous* this is described as a constant state of impending doom. We lose hope and become overwhelmed with anxiety. Yet our projections are seldom accurate. As Disraeli stated, "What we anticipate seldom occurs; what we least expect generally happens."

Typical Ways of Coping

Predictable ways of seeking to cope with anxiety can be readily identified. One frequently used method is *over-compliance.* We may seek to become people pleasers, always trying to meet the expectations of others. We may become what other people want us to become or we may imply that we agree with people when we do not as a means of gaining acceptance and relieving our anxiety. Thus, we become like the chameleon who changes his color to blend in with his environment.

Over-compliance results in loss of integrity.

When we adopt a life-style of over-compliance, we sacrifice our integrity. Integrity means wholeness. The word comes from the mathematical term *integer,* which is a number that isn't and cannot be divided. A person of integrity isn't divided against himself. He doesn't think one thing and say another. He doesn't believe one thing and do another. He is not in conflict with his own principles. Integrity is the absence of inner warfare, which enhances one's ability to act consistently.

Over-compliance diminishes the ability to establish our identity. The absence of consistency causes us to wonder who we are. In time, we come to be confused about who we are and what we stand for. Thus, anxiety is thereby increased.

Another method of dealing with anxiety is

withdrawal. As a way of dealing with anxiety, the person may retreat from the world and its problems. He runs from his perceived threats, although he is unable to escape from the accompanying apprehension. As one person stated, "Everywhere we go, we are there!"

Two dangers lurk with the person who handles anxiety in this fashion. First, becoming isolated, one tends to become separated from reality. Reality is the ability to see things clearly, as they are. While we seldom achieve completely accurate perceptions of reality, we fail to do it more so when we separate ourselves from other people who can give us the benefit of their perceptions. In isolation, anxiety grows, rather than diminishes. Second, the withdrawn person, with painful apprehensions of anxiety, is sometimes sorely tempted to medicate such anxiety and, thus, to withdraw even more. The anxiety is not halted; it is medicated so the person temporarily does not feel it so acutely.

The conflicts within a person are often acted out in relationships with others.

A third way of dealing with anxiety is through *aggression.* The conflicts within a person are acted out in relationships with others, frequently with the persons whom they love most. The anxious person may blame others for the conflicts within him. As he acts anxiously upon the world around him, it tends to respond in kind, thus escalating his anxiety.

From Anxiety to Security

Without being judgmental, we propose that anxiety is a failure of faith. It is often pathological; it contributes to numerous mental, emotional, and physical illnesses. Implicit in anxiety is the assumption that we must face the problems of life all alone. We tend to forget that God in His providential care will be present with us. Here are some suggestions to help us to move away from anxiety into the peace that comes through faith.

- Reflect on the times when you were anxious. You survived them, did you not? Most of our fears never actualize into reality. And, even if they do, God can use painful experiences for a good purpose. He alone can take a crucifixion and make a resurrection out of it.

- Own your anxieties. When we admit our anxieties, we are much more likely to get better than we are if we keep trying to block out disturbing thoughts. When we fail to own our anxieties, we are in denial — in the same manner of an alcoholic who cannot or does not face his drinking problem.

- Remember that not all anxiety is fatal. Some of it is normal, even though it may be painful. It is only when anxiety is prolonged and so intense that it continues to interfere with our daily functioning that it may be considered pathological. In such cases, a person should consult a professional counselor or a physician for help.

- Seek to identify the sources of your anxiety.

Sometimes we can do this easily; at other times it is difficult. It helps, however, to get your anxiety in focus so you can know what you are dealing with.

- Talk to God about the things you are anxious about. Practice Step 3. Turn your cares over to the care of God.

- Talk to yourself about your anxieties. It is not so much the events of life that affect us as it is our perceptions of those events. Can you "see" things in a way that will diminish your anxiety? It's worth a try.

- Talk about your anxiety in a support group. Group members often can help you put your worries in proper perspective. Even if they can't, talking about your anxiety often helps, because such talking causes you to face it. The very act of sharing our anxieties has the effect of helping us to release them, to stop trying to control them and to turn them loose. We cannot change anything unless we accept it. Denial does not liberate, it oppresses.

- Be aware that complete security is an illusion; none of us has it. The only security is God, who does not change and is willing to walk with us through our fears to the increase of our faith.

In conclusion, be aware that anxiety has a positive side. It does suggest that we are in touch with our intuitive power. If we felt no anxiety, we probably would be completely out of touch with reality. This antithesis is faith —

faith in a loving God who is ready to stand by us in all our stress.

*God, grant me the serenity to accept the things I
cannot change; the courage to change the things I
can; and the wisdom to know the difference.*

—*Reinhold Niebuhr*

*For every evil under the sun
There is a remedy or there is none;
If there be one, seek 'till you find it;
If there is none, never mind it.*

—*Anonymous*

10

From
Frustration
to
Serenity

"**I** am as frustrated as a termite in a yoyo," one person said. "Nothing seems to work out right." Most of us know how he felt, because everyone experiences frustration.

The word "frustration" derives from the Latin, *frustra,* meaning "in vain." It is a sense of insecurity or dissatisfaction that arises within a person because of unresolved problems, unfulfilled needs, or unachieved goals.

Sources of Frustration

One source of frustration is *unrealistic goals*. We desire something but discover that we are blocked from achieving it.

Joe had high goals -- so high, in fact, that he seldom reached them. He grew up being told that he was somebody special. What was given by his parents as an affirmation was received by him as a mandate to excel. He first heard the voices of his parents, but eventually heard the voice within himself that said, "You must be perfect, or else you are no good at all."

Unrealistic goals emerge out of the tendency toward perfectionism, the compulsive desire to not just do one's best, but to do things perfectly. Perfectionists live a no-win scenario. On the one hand, they are compelled to achieve; on the other hand, they set goals that are not achievable. Most perfectionists blame themselves for failure to achieve and continue to believe that the answer lies in striving toward even higher goals. The result is self-punishment through feelings of worthlessness, but perfectionism can never solve the problem of worthlessness because perfectionism *is* the problem of worthlessness.

A perfectionist often has difficulty accepting the unconditional love of God. He feels he must earn it.

A perfectionist often has difficulty in his spiritual life because he has difficulty accepting the unconditional love of God; he feels he must earn it. Thus, the perfectionist is trying to do the impossible; to earn the right to receive

God's love. Such cannot be done — and even if it could, grandiosity would probably emerge in one's life and block his relationship with God. The answer to perfectionism is found in accepting the grace of God. We will discuss this idea in greater detail in chapter 13.

A second source of frustration is *unpredicted circumstances* — events and happenings that interfere with our intentions.

The more we project into the future about how we think things should be, the more we will become frustrated because our expectations are likely to be shattered as things do not occur as we anticipated.

The phrase "One day at a time" is more than just a slogan; it is a therapeutic way of living that helps us lessen the frustration we may experience.

A third source of frustration is the *insatiable desire to control*. Such control may be expressed openly, but many times it is done covertly through manipulation. Manipulation is the attempt to control other people in subtle ways, to "hook" other people in ways that achieve from them a desired response. In essence, it is deceit.

The ways to manipulate are many: seeking to induce guilt, feigning helplessness, lavishing praise, or browbeating another person to elicit a desired response.

Manipulation is game-playing — and people who play games with other people usually confront situations where other people play games with them. Honesty in relationships becomes scarce, if, indeed, it exists at all. Hence, the manipulator creates an environment where people become untrustworthy.

People who grow up in extremely dysfunctional families often learn to manipulate in order to survive. In many cases, the manipulation continues long after the situation that contributed to it disappears.

The basic problem of the manipulator is spiritual. In essence, he is trying to be God. *Alcoholics Anonymous,* states, "First of all we had to quit playing God" (p. 69). If the manipulator does not openly claim to be God (and that very rarely happens), he will seek to control others and the world around him as if he is God. He will seek to use God for his own purposes. His prayers will be "deals" offered to God as attempts to extract favors to his own ends.

Responses to Frustration

Frustration is a painful feeling that demands a response, but we often make inappropriate responses.

One response to frustration is *aggression*, lashing out at others who may be completely innocent people and often the ones we love the most.

Open any daily newspaper in practically any major city and read the accounts of people who acted out aggressively because of their frustration. Bill W., co-founder of Alcoholics Anonymous, wrote:

> The chief activator of our defects has been self-centered fear—primarily fear that we would lose something we already possessed or would fail to get something we demanded. Living on a basis of unsatisfied demands, we were in a state of continual disturbance and

frustration. Therefore, no peace was to be had unless we could find a means of reducing the demands. (p. 22, *As Bill Sees It*).2

Another response to frustration is to *increase the attempt to control.* We dealt previously with the insatiable desire to control as a source of frustration. Ironically, for some people, the perceived answer to frustration is to do more of what caused the frustration in the first place. That is, they seek to control even more and, failing, experience an even greater degree of frustration. The sad part of this scenario is that the controlling person does not see that his deep need to control is not the answer, but the source, of his frustrating experiences in life.

For some people, the perceived answer to frustration is to do more of what caused the frustration in the first place.

A third response to frustration is the feeling of *fatalism,* in which a person, at least temporarily and sometimes permanently, gives up. Such is the tendency of the perfectionist, who tends to live with an "all or none" syndrome. "If I can't be perfect, I won't try at all. If I can't control everything, I'll just give up." Such statements illustrate the fatalistic attitude.

Another frequent response to frustration, which may occur simultaneously with those listed above, is to *medicate the frustration* with mood-altering chemicals. Regardless of the mood-altering chemical used, the desired affect is to feel differently. Since frustration is emotionally painful, attempts to diminish the pain in this manner is often done. The danger, however, is that through frequent use the person may become psychologically addicted. For the person in recovery, one response of this kind puts sobriety at risk, since the disease of addiction is permanent and progressive.

From Frustration to Serenity

While frustration is experienced by all persons, the addicted person seems to experience more of it and deal with it in less appropriate way. Looming large in the addicts life is the desire to stop drinking and the inability to do so.

The opposite of frustration is serenity. It refers to an inner quietness. That word "serenity" does not, as such, appear in the Bible. However, the word "peace" does appear, and it means the same thing. It is not life without conflict, but the ability to remain calm and secure in the midst of conflict. The word "peace" appears in the Bible frequently with the word "grace," which refers to the unmerited gift of God to us. It seems the biblical writers were saying that there is no peace except by the grace of God. Thus, serenity is not something we work up; rather it is something we pray down.

- What are your goals? Few of us have them explicitly stated; more frequently they are implicit. Nevertheless, they are there. Are they realistic? Are they your goals, or goals that someone else indicated you should have? Goals give direction to life. However, if our goals are unrealistic, we will feel the constant pressure of frustration.

- Are you trying to control things that are beyond your control. Are you trying to be God. Learn to "Let go and let God."

- Focus on changing the things you can change. Don't waste your energy on the impossible.

- Ask God to grant you wisdom to know what you should try to change and what you should let go.

In conclusion, reducing frustration can be done in two ways. First, we seek to avoid those things that frustrate us. Second, we learn to cope with frustration in a more effective manner. Complete avoidance of frustration is impossible and learning to deal with frustration in appropriate ways is a sure sign of growth toward maturity.

Friendship is born at that moment when one person says to another, 'What! You, too? I thought I was the only one.'

—C. S. Lewis

11

From
Loneliness
to
Intimacy

There was a pall of loneliness in her eyes as she talked. "I know lots of people," she said, "but I don't know any of them very well. I seem to move from one world of relationships to another. Recently, I have been moving more away from people and more into drinking."

The factors contributing to increased loneliness are many. Increased mobility among people makes it difficult for them to stay in one location and "put down roots." Changing lifestyles make a sense of community difficult to attain. Fast paces and busy schedules cover our loneliness, but also contribute to it. When there is a pause, many people discover that they live in haunted houses — houses

97

occupied with the ghosts of loneliness. Like Mr. McGoo we lament:

> You don't know how it feels when you talk,
> And nobody's voice talks back.
> A hand for each hand was planned for the world;
> Why don't the fingers reach?
> Millions of grains of sand in the world;
> Why such a lonely beach?
> Where is a voice to answer mine back,
> Where are two shoes to click to my clack?
> I'm all alone in the world.[1]

Sometimes people drink or use other mood-altering drugs because they feel lonely, only to discover that such action contributes to their loneliness.

The Need to Belong

The need to belong is both instinctual and learned. We begin life with the basic instinct to relate to others. That instinct is nurtured, and the need to belong grows stronger as we mature. Unfortunately, our skills in relating to people do not always keep pace with our need to belong. Everyone wants to belong, but many people just don't know how to go about it.

Every person needs love and acceptance from others. William Glasser in *Reality Therapy* states that every person needs at least one other person who loves him and accepts him if he is to meet his emotional needs.[2] The paradox is this: If we seek to make people love us we usually drive them away from us. Some people, in an effort to get people to love them, become notorious love-seekers. They become what C. S. Lewis, in his book, *Four*

Loves, calls "...those pathetic people who simply want friends and can never make any."

Alcoholics Anonymous describes very succinctly the plight of loneliness as it relates to the addicted person:

> He cannot picture life without alcohol. Some day he will be unable to imagine life either with alcohol or without it. Then he will know loneliness such as few do. He will be at the jumping-off place. He will wish for the end (p. 152).

Levels of Belonging

Intimacy, the sharing of life on a deep level, is not possible with all people. To seek intimacy with all people may result in not achieving a close relationship with anyone.

Our interpersonal relationships may be classified into four categories. First, we must face the unfortunate fact that with some people we will probably never develop positive relationships. We should be cautious, however, to assure that we do not relinquish our responsibility to be kind to such people. Circumstances change and people change. Thus, the relationship may also change.

Second, it is appropriate for us to nourish a genuine desire to help humankind as if we were all members of one family. Following the death of F. Scott Fitzgerald there was found among his private papers a list of themes from which he intended to some day write short stories. One of them read, "Suggestions for a story — A widely separated family inherits a house in which they must learn to live together." The idea was not original to Fitzgerald. We have inherited a house from God, the world. All people must live in it.

Third, each of us has his own world of relationships, the network of people with whom we come in contact in the normal course of daily activities. Many of them are acquaintances; some of them are friends.

Finally, each person needs a world of intimate relationships, people with whom intimate things may be shared confidentially. The people in this world know us for who we are, both our strengths and our weaknesses, and accept us — often not because of them, but in spite of them. The intimate world of relationships is painfully small for some people. For others, including the alcoholic or addict, it is practically nonexistent.

When we enlarge our intimate world, we increase our feelings of belonging and diminish our feelings of loneliness.

The extent to which we can enlarge the intimate world affects our feelings of belonging and diminishes our feelings of loneliness. Herein is one of the primary values of a support group, such as Alcoholics Anonymous. In support groups, members can share intimate feelings in confidence. Such support groups exists for a wide array of issues and problems. Many of them are based on the 12 steps.

Loneliness as Phoniness

Loneliness increases when we choose to relate to

people in less authentic or more superficial ways. The person who seems unable to find the courage to be himself experiences deep feelings of loneliness.

A great deal of effort is spent by people seeking to relate in these less authentic ways. In an effort to belong they will either consciously or unconsciously play games. Such games are numerous, but a few deserve to be mentioned.

- *Self-depreciation*, in which a person exhibits false humility, hoping that the other person will respond with a compliment.

- *Self-righteousness,* in which the person secretly hopes he will be admired for his goodness.

- *Overcompliance,* in which a person believes others will like him because he is so agreeable and never causes any trouble.

- *Martyrdom,* in which a person hopes he will be admired for all his sacrifices.

- *Intellectualism,* in which a person seeks to demonstrate how brilliant he is, thinking that anyone as smart as he perceives himself to be is bound to be accepted.

Do you know some games people play to hide their real self? You probably could add to this list.

People do not always play these games to intentionally be deceitful; they play them because they somehow cannot give themselves permission just to be themselves.

The Pursuit of Intimacy

Intimacy is grasping the internal world of another person. It is the quality or condition of being close to other people. It is seldom a unilateral experience; it is an experience mutually shared by two or more people.

Intimacy begins with *self-awareness.* When a person is in touch with himself, he is more conscious of his needs and motivations. His denial system is less active and he can be more authentic. The less one is in touch with his inner feelings, the more likely he will seek to manipulate other people. The question is, How does a person work to be in touch with himself? One way is to learn to "check in."

> The magic words of checking in are "how" and "what." How am I belonging to this person right now? What is the extra message I may be sending? Am I pitifully pouting, burrowing into his heart, and gouging a chunk of compassion for his acceptance of me? Am I coercing him with my stabbing sarcasm to think as I think? Am I belly-laughing at mediocre jokes to extract the approval of the joke teller? Am I being super-agreeable to keep him glued to me? Am I straining to find out what he expects of me so I can comply, thus buying his acceptance of me? Am I displaying how helpless I am, milking his help?[5]

Simply stated, checking in is learning to perceive yourself objectively, getting "outside yourself" to see yourself as you think others may see you. Checking in is a skill that can be developed and improved. At first, you may be overwhelmed with the fact that you have been deceiving yourself by not checking in previously, but you will begin to learn more about your own needs—needs which you may have subtly attempted to manipulate other people to fulfill.

A corollary to checking in is checking out. Checking out is the process of receiving feedback from persons with whom you relate. Checking out helps us to determine if we are indeed communicating to others what we think we are communicating.

> Talk exists on at least three levels of meaning: (1) What the speaker is saying; (2) What the speaker thinks he is saying, and (3) What the listener thinks he is saying. The first level requires little consideration. The second and third levels require more consideration than the first. Here is where the differences may arise; while the speaker thinks he is being understood on one level, the listener may be listening on an entirely different level.[4]

Checking out may be achieved in two ways. First, there is nonverbal feedback. What do I sense about the way the other person responds to my message? Do I sense anxiety? anger? fear? boredom? joy? acceptance? Second, ask the other person to give you feedback on how you are coming across? Such verbal feedback will often be given if the other person feels relatively certain that you will receive it and learn from it.

Intimacy with other people is more likely achieved when we *claim ownership* of our thoughts, feelings, and actions. Ownership means that we do not blame others for them. For example, we don't say, "You frustrate me." Rather, we say, "I am frustrated." The other person may be responsible for the action, but you are responsible for your feeling of frustration.

> Of course, we feel better assigning our emotions
> to other people. You made me angry ... you
> made me jealous ... you frightened me.... The
> fact is that you can't make me anything. You
> can only stimulate the emotions that are already
> in me, waiting to be activated. The distinction
> between causing and stimulating the emotion is
> not just a play on words. If I think you can make
> me angry, I simply lay the blame and pin the
> problem on you. I can then walk away from our
> encounter learning nothing, concluding that
> you were at fault because you made me angry.
> Then I need to ask no questions of myself be-
> cause I have laid all the responsibility at your
> feet.[5]

Intimacy with other people is better achieved when
we are willing *to be open;* to share with other people our
honest feelings and not cover them up. John Powell in his
book, *The Secret of Staying in Love,* points out two ways to
communicate with people. One way is *discussion;* the act
of telling others factual information. The other type of
communication is *dialogue.* Dialogue is sharing feelings,
hopes, and dreams - those thoughts and feelings that come
from the core of our being. Dialogue is one way we
express openness.

Openness is essential to intimacy because intimacy
demands knowledge. We cannot be intimate with people
we do not know and people cannot be intimate with us
unless they know who we are.

Empathy is another essential quality of intimacy.
Empathy is the process of placing oneself in the frame of
reference of another, feeling the world as he feels it,
sharing his world with him. Empathy requires that we cast
off the cloak of judgment. That is, we do not pass judg-

ment on what we discover when we enter the frame of reference of another person.

> I suggest that each of us discovered that this kind of understanding is extremely rare. We never receive nor offer it with great frequency. Instead, we offer another type of understanding which is different, such as, 'I understand what is wrong with you' or 'I understand what makes you that way.' These are types of understandings which we usually offer and receive - evaluative understanding from the outside. It is not surprising that we shy away from true understanding. If I am truly open to the way life is experienced by another person—if I can take his world into mine - then I run the risk of seeing life in his way, of being changed myself, and we all resist change.[6]

Thus, the primary requirement for developing empathy is the willingness to change ourselves, if necessary, rather than to insist that other people change to become like us.

From Loneliness to Intimacy

Loneliness is deeply rooted in fear — fear of not being accepted for who we are. The answer to loneliness is to begin to cultivate intimate friends.

- Examine how you tend to relate to other people. Do you gouge them for approval? Such gouging does not go unnoticed and frequently causes people to move away from you rather than toward you.

- Seek to be more open with people about how you feel. People cannot love you unless you are willing to let them know who you are. Own your feelings. Do not attribute them to someone else. Someone else may have committed an act that prompted your feelings, but the feelings are distinctly yours. Do not assign responsibility for them to someone else.

- Be generous with sincere compliments. Remember that you are not the only needy person in the world. Other people need love and affirmation too.

- Learn to listen to other people. Show sincere interest in their concerns. You will be surprised at the interest other people will show toward you if you are willing to listen to them, rather than doing all the talking.

- Establish a home support group; a group of people with whom you meet regularly. It takes time to cultivate intimate friends and a home group will provide you this time.

- Be certain that you have a sponsor in your recovery. That person should be among your most intimate friends, the person you can call when you need to talk about a problem.

Once you take the initiative to make friends, you may discover that you have lots of company when it comes to loneliness. Other people are lonely also, and often waiting for you to take the first step in establishing a relationship.

Notes

1. "Mr. McGoo's Christmas Carol": N.B.C., 1964

2. William Glasser, *Reality Therapy* (New York: Harper & Row, Publishers, 1965).

3. W. W. Broadbent, *How to Be Loved* (Englewood Cliffs: Prentice Hall, 1976), pp. 51-52.

4. Gerald I. Nierenberg and Henry H. Calerno, *Meta-Talk: Guide to Hidden Meanings in Communication* (New York: Trident Press, 1974), pp. 16-17.

5. John Powell, *The Secret of Staying in Love* (Niles, IL: Argus Communications, 1976), p. 96.

6. Carl Rogers, *Person to Person: The Problem of Being Human* (Lafayette, CA: Real People Press, 1967), pp. 92-94.

Is not dread of thirst when your well is full the thirst that is unquenchable?

—Gibran

If a person needs a million acres to make him feel rich, and if he's poor in hisself, there ain't no million acres gonna make him feel rich, an' maybe he's disappointed that nothin' he can do'll make him feel rich.

—John Steinbeck, The Grapes of Wrath

12

From
Greed
to
Generosity

If you had everything you ever wanted, would it be enough? For many people it would not. John D. Rockefellow, a noted philanthropist, was asked, "How much money does it take for a person to be satisfied?" He replied, "Just a little more."

Few of us would be willing to openly admit that we are greedy. Yet all of us are — and some of us more than others.

What Is Greed?

Greed masquerades itself in many forms. It is subtle and expresses itself in many ways.

First, greed frequently appears as *ambition*. Kevin grew up in a poor family. He remembered and shared with embarrassment how he ate welfare lunches at school. His clothes were hand-me-downs that were originally worn by his older brother. Kevin never invited friends to his house because he felt ashamed for them to see the small, unpainted, poorly maintained dwelling where he lived.

Kevin's brothers and sisters grew up to a lifestyle that perpetuated the cycle of poverty, as often is the case. But Kevin responded differently. Although he almost dropped out of high school, he did graduate, something no other family member had ever done. Moreover, Kevin enrolled in college, taking a full study load while maintaining a part-time job to pay his tuition and living expenses.

Except for some latent jealousy from his siblings, Kevin was continually affirmed by community and family members for his ambition and achievements.

Upon graduation from college, Kevin landed a job with a good corporation. He was perceived by the corporate leaders as being ambitious and competitive, qualities they held in high esteem. In a few years, Kevin was promoted to middle management. The corporation made due demands on Kevin, but his self-imposed demands were greater. By this time, he was accustomed to a continuous striving for more and more. In the words of Wayne Oates, he had become a workaholic.

> Workaholism is a word I have invented. It means addiction to work, the compulsion or uncontrollable need to work incessantly. Workaholism has hidden beginnings in economic, cultural, and emotional deprivations in childhood.

> Overworking is often an expression of greed. It is prompted by the feeling that enough is not sufficient and sufficiency is not enough. [1]

It is not our intent to indict ambition. Rather, we refer to compulsive work that happens to the extent that it creates noticeable mental disturbances or interferes with bodily health, personal happiness, interpersonal relations, and smooth social functioning.

Second, greed often expresses itself in *selfish behavior*. While greed is frequently used to refer to material possessions, it is related to more than material goods. The person may be greedy in his expectations of others. Such greed is equivalent to selfishness.

Few people deliberately set out to be selfish. More often, they are needy and their selfish behavior is an attempt to meet their needs. In fact, a person who is critically needy is practically incapable of being unselfish. He cannot stand in another person's shoes because his own feet hurt so badly. Like a person with a throbbing toothache, he cannot listen to another person tell about his pain.

Our needs can be clearly identified; the problem arises in how we attempt to meet our needs and the extent to which our attempts are successful. Abraham Maslow, noted psychologist, identified humankind's needs as a heirarchy (see p. 112)[2]

We all have a need for *survival*. Someone has described a newborn child as a glob of protoplasm with a ravaging appetite on one end and a total sense of irresponsibility on the other. The newborn must have at least one person to meet his need for survival. Eventually, the

The Self   **The Addict**

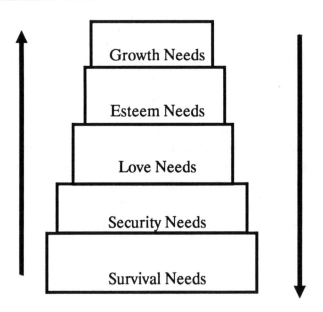

MASLOW'S PYRAMID AND ADDICTION

The healthy self seeks to move up to meeting higher needs. In contrast, the addictive self tends to move in the opposite direction, thus creating conflicts within the person.

person grows to the point where he becomes responsible for his own survival. When his survival is threatened, the person becomes very needy.

The next level of need is related to *security*. We not only want to survive, but we also want to make our world secure. Security is often sought through resistance to change, because change often threatens our security.

The two needs described above, survival and security, are basic. Until we have those needs met in a relatively satisfactory manner, we usually do not give much attention to other needs. However, once we have survival and security needs under control, we can move to other needs. The next need is for *love and belonging*. The activities we engage in to meet these needs are many, among which are marriage, joining clubs and organizations, and socializing in other ways. We need to feel that we belong to other people and that they belong to us.

The next need is for *esteem — self-esteem and the esteem of others*. We need to feel good about ourselves and to feel that other people consider us to be worthwhile or significant.

Finally, we have a need to *grow* — to become all that we can be. The growth need is inherent in us, but it can be stifled. And, we usually do not concentrate on it much until we have the lower needs met in a relatively satisfactory way.

As we meet our own needs, we become more capable of unselfish living.

As we meet our needs, we become more capable of

unselfish living. When we fail to meet our needs, we tend to become selfish, unable to help others because we feel so needy.

In addiction, the person discovers that he has conflicting urges. The self wants to survive, be secure, love and belong, experience self-esteem and the esteem of others, and grow toward his potential. Addictive behavior that ensues from the use of mood-altering chemicals does just the opposite. A civil war rages within that can only be stopped through halting the use of the chemicals. Frustration sets in because most addicted persons cannot alone stop the intake of the chemicals that are destroying happiness and, ultimately, life itself. This is where the 12 step program is applicable. Recovering people involved in 12 step programs have discovered other ways to meet their needs that do not include the use of mood-altering chemicals.

The practicing addict becomes selfish because he is needy.

The practicing addict becomes selfish because he is needy. In addiction, growth stops, esteem diminishes, love and belonging are not experienced in a normal fashion, security becomes fragile, and, ultimately, survival fails. The 12 step program provides a way for people to meet their needs without the use of mood-altering chemicals. It helps the person to stop the downward trend and to get life in a growth pattern, rather than a decline.

Third, greed expresses itself as *covetousness and envy.* Covetousness is the desire to possess something that belongs to someone else. Envy is the resentful and hateful dislike of the good fortune of other people. When harbored within us, covetousness and envy poison our perception of the good life. When it is acted out, it often brings negative consequences in the lives of all persons associated with it.

Finally, greed is all of the things listed above, but basically, *greed is about fear.* The motivating force behind greed is fear of deprivation. The greedy person seeks more and more, not necessarily because he enjoys his seeking or his attainment, but primarily because he is afraid he will not have enough. Gibran wrote, "Is not dread of thirst when your well is full, the thirst that is unquenchable." Augustine spoke of this fear when he wrote, "Greed suggests to the mind a lengthy old age, inability to perform manual labor at some future date, famines that are sure to come, sickness that will visit us, the pinch of poverty, the great shame that comes from accepting the necessities of life from others."

The insatiable quest for more and more can leave a person feeling empty and unable to enjoy what he has.

The insatiable quest for more and more can leave a person feeling empty and unable to enjoy what he has. John Steinbeck expressed the concept adequately in *The Grapes of Wrath* when he had one of his characters to state that "If a person needs a million acres to make him feel rich, and if he's poor in hisself, there ain't no million acres gonna make him feel rich, an' maybe he's disappointed that nothin' he can do'll make him feel rich."

What Greed Does

The consequences of greed are easily identified. *First, greed is a spiritual problem. It separates a person from his Higher Power.* The greedy person has his own selfish agenda. If he prays, it usually is an attempt to manipulate God to meet his own needs.

Second, greed *alienates us from other people,* often from the people we love the most. People become objects to be used to meet one's selfish ends.

Third, *greed contributes to stress that can have physical effects.* Driven by fear, the person may make undue demands on his physical energy until it fails, resulting in physical illness. Because of the emotional discomfort associated with greed, the person may begin to medicate that discomfort, resulting in addictive behavior.

From Greed to Generosity

Are you a victim of your own greed? Here are some questions to answer and steps to take to move toward generosity.

- Do you enjoy the money and possessions you already have? Or do you neglect to enjoy them because you are so busy trying to get more? If so, you may be obsessed with getting, rather than living.

- Reflect on what you have. Remember when you didn't have it, how much you wanted it, and how hard you worked to get it? Are you enjoying it?

116

Taking it for granted while you push on for more? If so, more probably will not be enough.

- Do you own your possessions, or do they own you? What are the actual pleasures and meanings you get from them? Are they worth the amount of time, energy, and anxiety you spend trying to acquire and maintain them?

- Drop the fantasy that rich people are always happier. They just have more money; they may not be happy. They may just be dealing with their problems in a fancier setting.

- Do you give attention to how to manage your possessions? There are never enough resources to adequately supply bad management. Conversely, good management helps us to realize that we often can be happy with less. If you have continuous difficulty with finances, perhaps you should become involved in Debtors Anonymous.

- Are you neglecting your interpersonal relationships in an effort to acquire more things? Dedicate yourself to building up all your assets, including the ones money can't buy, such as health, capacity to love, appreciation of life. Learn to be grateful for your blessings. That way, if you do get rich you will already know how to enjoy it and if you don't, you will be too busy living to notice.

- Trust God to supply your needs. Live for him. Remember the biblical injunction, "I once was young, but now I am old; yet I have never seen the children of the righteous hungering for bread"(Ps. 37:25).

A very wealthy man died. Someone asked, "How much money did he leave." The reply: "He left it all!"

Long ago the Bible instructed us that a persons life does not consist of the abundance of his possessions.

Notes

1. Wayne E. Oates, *Confessions of A Workaholic* (Nashville: Abingdon Press, 1971), p. 1.

2. Abraham Maslow, *Motivation and Personality* (New York: Harper and Brothers, 1954).

If we are painstaking about this phase of our development, we will be amazed before we are half through. We will suddenly realize that God is doing for us what we could not do for ourselves. . . .

—*Alcoholics Anonymous, pp. 83-84*

Amazing Grace, how sweet the sound
That saved a wretch like me.
I once was lost but now I'm found
Was blind but now I see.

—*John Newton*

13

From
Self-Reliance
to
Grace

The 12 step program is frequently referred to as a "self-help" program. It can more adequately be described as a "God-help" program. The big book of *Alcoholics Anonymous* states, "We will suddenly realize that God was doing for us what we could not do for ourselves." This loving action in our lives can be appropriately referred to as God's grace.

What Is Grace?

Grace is perhaps the most beautiful word in our spiritual vocabulary. It comes from the Greek, *charis,* meaning a gift. Its origin is in Eastern tradition of biblical times. When an Eastern ruler wanted to make his people happy, he would provide them a gift, known as charis. It was not something that was earned or had to be repaid. It was not manipulated by the recipients; rather, it was freely given by the ruler. As such, there was always joy and gratitude associated with it. Biblical writers used this analogy when referring to what God has done and is doing for us. God provides charis, or grace to us. Just as in the case of the Eastern ruler and his people, we cannot earn it, repay it, or manipulate it. We can only choose to receive it or to reject it.

In previous chapters of this book we have given attention to the feelings that form a wall between us and God. This wall of feelings frequently cuts us off from receiving God's grace, not because it is not offered, but because we either will not or cannot receive it.

- *Grandiosity leads us to think that we do not need God's grace.*

- *Guilt leads us to assume that we are not worthy of grace.*

- *Grief can lead us to think that God's grace is no longer offered.*

- *Resentment causes a wall of anger that keeps us from experiencing God's love — His grace.*

- *Self-pity, likewise, causes us to doubt if God's grace is available to us.*

- *Anxiety assumes that we must handle life's problems alone, for which we feel inadequate.*

- *Frustration comes often from trying to rely on our own power rather than the grace of God.*

- *Loneliness cuts us off from other people, thus thwarting God's use of other people as grace messengers to us.*

- *Greed causes us to focus on our fears and inadequacies, rather than seeking to access God's grace in our lives.*

All of these efforts are attempts at self-sufficiency, at trying to depend on ourselves, rather than accessing and relying on the grace of God.

How Grace Comes

Access to grace is achieved in two ways. First, we achieve it through faith. Step 2 states:

> Came to believe that a Power greater than ourselves can restore us to sanity.

While that involves believing in the existence of God, it also involves more; it means that we come to believe that God is willing and will help us. Second, we demonstrate that faith through willingness. In other words, after we come to believe that God is willing to help us, we become willing to allow him to do so. Such willingness is more than a mere affirmation; it is a demonstration. That is, we begin to cooperate with God so that his grace may be experienced in our lives. We posture ourselves humbly before God so that His grace can become a conscious reality.

God's grace is given to us in any way that God

chooses. After all, He is God and can dispense His grace as he chooses. *Frequently, however, grace manifests itself through people with whom we come in contact.* God has called us to live in the community. That has been true since the beginning of time when He said, "It is not good that man should live alone" (Gen. 2:18). In the 12 step program, this reality is frequently experienced by people who hear at meetings the very things they need to hear most. When a person continues to attend meetings, he postures himself to receive God's grace. When he isolates, he alienates himself from God's grace and is at risk of relapse.

Grace also works through circumstances. God is both within us and above us. Being above us, he controls circumstances. As the poet has said, "God moves in mysterious ways, His wonders to perform." In the midst of painful circumstances, it is sometimes difficult for us to experience God's grace. However, looking back, we often see that His grace was operating even when we did not know it.

What Grace Does

First, grace provides protection. We have heard testimonials from recovering persons about how by all realistic expectations they should no longer be alive. Auto accidents, attempted suicides, loss of desire to live — these and more incidents are told by recovering people. Their survival is attributed to God's grace that was operating to protect them.

Second, grace empowers us to do what we cannot do by ourselves. The biblical word for power is *dunamis,* from which we derive our word dynamite. *Dunamis* is the power that raises the dead, as demonstrated in the resurrection of Jesus. When one follows Step 1 and admits that he does not have within himself the power to arrest addiction and its ensuing destructive behavior, he postures himself to stop relying on his own power and to rely on the power of God.

Third, grace gives us the ability to persevere. So long as we posture ourselves in humility before God and remain willing, His grace is experienced to help maintain sobriety and sanity. Conversely, when we get out of the appropriate posture – and that is done primarily when grandiosity and self-sufficiency begin to operate in our lives – we cut ourselves off from receiving God's grace and are at risk of relapse. Terrance Gorski, in *Staying Sober*, reminds us that relapse happens within the persons thinking and feeling processes before the person actually consumes mood-altering chemicals. Through humility and continued willingness, God's grace continues to operate in our sobriety.

Finally, grace moves us toward our potential. We discover that we are growing again, something that stopped in our addiction.

The direction of our growth is toward Godlikeness. What is God doing in our lives? What does he want? He wants us to become like him – not to be Him, as many have tried to do in their addiction – but to become like Him. Therein is the greatest source of meaningfulness and happiness that the human being can achieve. Therein is freedom – freedom from grandiosity, guilt, grief, frustration — all the maladies of mind and hindrances of the heart that keep us from experiencing abundant life.

From Self-Reliance to Grace

How do we increase our sensitivity to God's grace? In the interest of simplicity, we use the word **D-A-I-L-Y** as graphically illustrated page 141. Grace is as close as one's hand. The following five activities can help us to be more sensitive and receptive to God's grace.

- **DEVOTE** time to meditation. Meditation is getting in touch with our feelings. Often it comes freely through quietness and reflection. In such moments, we can experience the presence and power of God. Sometimes we need help to put us into the proper posture for meditation. Whatever turns our thoughts toward the Infinite can be a springboard for meditation.

  For some, it is a book of readings, such as *24 Hours a Day*. Others find help in the Bible. Such passages as Psalm 23 provide occasions for reflection on the power and providence of God. The key idea is to take some time each day to look inward to ourselves and upward to our Creator.

  Being in close contact with nature is another help found by some people. Public worship with other people helps some people to set the stage for their private meditation. Any or all of these activities — and perhaps many others — can be occasions for one to contemplate the Infinite, to experience the presence of a Higher Power.

  Discipline is frequently needed to engage in meditation. We suggest the following.

(1) *Find a suitable place.* The nature of the place may vary with people, but the important thing is to find your listening point and go there regularly.
(2) *Set a definite time.* If you miss the time one day, don't despair and stop. Just get back on schedule.
(3) *Begin by spending a brief time in an activity to prepare you for meditation.* Read, offer a prayer, call to remembrance a quotation, appreciate the beauty of God's world — do whatever is necessary and helpful to transcend the daily cares and to meditate on the goodness and grace of God.
(4) *Pray for understanding and guidance.* Then just be still and listen. Let the presence of God fill you. Let Him have free access to your thoughts.
(5) *Close your meditation with a paraphrase of Steps 1, 2, and 3.* "God, I'm powerless over many things, but I believe you can help me. I turn these things over to your care."

- **ALWAYS PRAY.** Do it every day. Meditation and prayer are inseparable. Thus, most of what was mentioned above relates to prayer. Your prayers may be formal or informal; public or private. The main thing is that we engage in it daily. The various aspects of prayer may be used separately or together, so long as they are done in a spirit of humility.
  (1) Acknowledge the greatness and goodness of God.
  (2) Pray for greater knowledge of His will and the power to carry it out.

(3) Relinquish those things you are powerless over; put them into the care of God and be willing to do the next right thing as it is revealed to you. Let the wisdom of God guide you in your actions.
(4) Pray for God's will for today, realizing that He will still be with you tomorrow. This is a part of living one day at a time.
(5) Ask for God's forgiveness and the willingness to forgive others whom you may resent.
(6) Ask God to protect you from evil; to help you to stay sober each day.
Don't be too concerned about using the "right" words. Remember that prayer is the sincere desire of the heart.

- **INVOLVE YOURSELF WITH OTHERS.** *Recovery is personal, but it is never private.* Involvement with others is necessary. The benefits of such involvement are many. In times of spiritual need, God has a way of directing us to the proper resources if we are willing. These resources often come in the form of other people who can give us counsel and encouragement. Remember, God's grace frequently comes to us in this manner. When we cut ourselves off from other people, we may diminish our sensitivity to God's grace. Moreover, other people become mirrors that reflect to us that which we are not able to see when we are alone.
The person who cannot acknowledge the need for help is stoking the fire of a burning ego. He is at risk that the fire will rage out of control. People need people. Involvement with others also gives

us the opportunity to share our love, counsel, and encouragement with others. Hence, we may become the instruments of God's grace to others.

- **LIVE THE 12 STEPS.** The 12 steps are not just about alcohol, the malady for which they were originally written; they are about living. They provide a viable way for a person to get his emotional and spiritual needs met. In order to grow emotionally and spiritually, we must develop an intimate relationship with God. Such intimacy can be nurtured by living the 12 steps.

- **YIELD YOURSELF TO GOD.** To admit powerlessness does not leave a person without hope. Powerlessness helps us to stop depending on ourselves and to relinquish ourselves to God. Paradoxically, the surrendered person discovers a new sense of power, the power of God.

All we have to offer God is ourselves — and that is all he wants. The slogan "Let go and let God" is another way of expressing the need to relinquish ourselves to God. For the relinquishment to be effective, it must be complete.

For by grace are you saved through faith, and not that of yourselves; it is a gift of God. (Eph. 2:8)

Guidelines for Group Meetings

Environment

The first consideration should be to secure a suitable location. Following are suggestions regarding physical surroundings.

1. Try to secure a large room with plenty of table space, as free as possible from distractions. We like the idea of sitting at a table because it makes it easier to take notes.

2. Many people shy away from meetings where there is smoking. When possible secure a smoke-free environment. Ideally, you could provide both a smokers' and non-smokers' meeting.

3. We prefer a circle type seating arrangement whenever possible. This provides the speaker and the listerners with eye contact.

4. A small group provides each member with a greater chance to establish intimacy and trust. Eight to 12 members is an optimum size. Smaller groups tend to increase competitiveness and defensiveness. Larger groups become impersonal and may allow some persons to get lost in the crowd.

5. Since some activities may require writing, provide pencils and paper for those who may be unprepared.

About Group Leadership

1. The group leader should assume responsibility for securing the meeting place, making provisions for refreshments, and providing extra pencils/paper. (Always try to leave the meeting place looking better than it did when you arrived.)

2. The group leader should be responsible for initiating the meeting and for steering the discussion in the proper direction, keeping members on task.

The group leader should take special care to provide an atmosphere conducive to sharing, encouraging open discussion.

4. The group leader should refrain from making judgmental statements and/or gestures.

5. The group leader should encourage members to participate by modeling appropriate behavior.

6. The group leader should facilitate the opening and closing of the meeting by requiring prayer, choral reading, etc. He may delegate such reponsibility. It is generally best to agree upon an established routine, such as the Lord's Prayer, the Serenity Prayer, etc.

7. The group leader should encourage members to keep a prayer list of those participating in the group.

8. The group leader should clarify the group's purpose prior to actually beginning group work.

Should the group leader be a person involved in personal recovery? Should leadership be elected? Should the leadership position be rotated each quarter? These are questions which are best decided locally. Whatever the case, it should be abundantly clear that the leader's primary purpose is not to judge comments or to lecture all the time; the leader's purpose is to serve. The group's purpose should be extablished prior to commencement by the membership. Any time it appears that the group is straying away from its intended purpose as so expressed by its membership, new leadership should be considered.

Sharpening Listening Skills

The group relationship will be highly enhanced when the membership seeks to communicate effectively and efficiently. Effective communication involves listening as well as speaking. The relationship between the speaker and the listener is strengthened when both show understanding of the feeling and content of the speaker. Effective listening as a tool of communication is useful also because it forces the listener out of himself/herself. Often it is this "self as center" that keeps a person from communicating at all.

Basically, there are two types of listening, passive and active. Passive listeners keep most of what is said and may even acknowledge what is said, but usually exhibit nonverbal messages of disinterest. Active listeners usually not only understand what is being said, but can identify feelings as well.

Effective listening requires time. A patient listener rarely interrupts the speaker and does not begin planning a response while speaking is taking place. Effective listeners are non-judgmental. They are empathetic. They participate in the feelings of the speaker. Effective listeners are aware of nonverbal clues which express open-ness and honesty

Member Participation

1. The members should avoid judgmental statement and/or gestures.

2. The members should avoid self-serving criticism.

3. The members should concern themselves primarily with self-therapy and refrain from unnecessary giving of advice.

4. The members should be open and honest regarding feelings.

5. The members should be active participants, whether it involves talking or being active listeners.

6. The members should always honor confidentiality.

7. The members should respect the rights of others.

8. The members should share responsibility for maintaining the physical facilities.

Confidentiality

Confidentiality must be assured if group therapy is to be effective. Trust is very difficult to establish. Once it has been violated it is virtually impossible to re-instate. Confidentiality and respect for the privacy of others shall be of utmost priority, particularly outside the meeting place.

Chapter 1: Spirituality: The Power and the Process

1. Define spirituality. What is your concept of the term?

2. Review the terms pluralism and tolerance. Raise this question: How might we conduct our meetings so that we encourage openness and allow for individual differences?

3. Share a list of "do's" and "don'ts" based upon your previous religious/spiritual training.

4. Discuss experiences and events which create a wall of separation between yourself and God.

5. Review the wall of feelings charted in this chapter. There are nine negative feelings discussed. Choose one of the feelings and relate an experience involving that feeling and tell what you have done or what you are doing to turn the negative feeling into a positive one.

Chapter 2: From Alienation to Conscious Contact

1. How and for what do you pray? When and where do you pray?

2. From your experiences, how does God answer prayer?

3. Locate and discuss the five basic assumptions about God discussed in this chapter. What assumptions mean the most to you.

4. What is unconditional love? From whom have you experienced it?

5. Have you ever tried to bargain with God? What were the results?

6. Read together the third step prayer. How is this passage speaking for you and to you today?

7. Think of praying as writing a letter to God. Write a letter to God regarding an issue you are dealing with. Remember to use everday language and to write about your feelings. Share your letter with the group.

Chapter 3: From Self-Depreciation to Self-Esteem

1. "History is filled with records of many sensible people who have chosen to die in dignity rather than to live in shame." What does this statement mean to you?

2. Are your feelings of low self-esteem due to your addiction, or is your addiction due to your feelings of low self-esteem? What is the relationship between the two?

3. Describe your view of God. Is it one of God as cruel and judgmental or is it one of God as kind, loving, and forgiving? Why do you view God in the manner you do?

4. Freud advocated that pleasure was the primary motive for our actions. Adler advocated that all of man's activities could be explained as the will to power. What are the primary motives for your actions?

5. What does it mean to fear God? Are we supposed to be afraid of God?

6. "Meaning comes when a person is satisfied with himself." How is this statement speaking to you? Is it ever possible to be fully satisfied with oneself?

7. How does addiction rob us of self-esteem?

8. Review the esteem triangle illustrated in this chapter. What does it mean to you?

9. "We live our way into patterns of thinking and feeling more frequently than we think or feel our way into patterns of living." What does this statement mean to you?

10. Review the suggestions at the end of this chapter. Share impressions with one another.

Chapter 4: From Grandiosity to Humility

1. Charles Lindbergh said the success of his flight was due to the proper altitude. What does this mean in terms of grandiosity and humility?

2. What is grandiosity? How does a grandiose attitude affect our relationships to others and to God?

3. "Grandiose behavior often is a camouflage for fear." How does this statement speak to you today?

4. Review each of the suggestions at the end of this chapter. Share how you can use them in daily life.

Chapter 5: From Guilt to Forgiveness

1. You will need paper and pencil for this activity. Draw two vertical lines on a sheet of paper, forming three columns. In the first column, list 10 basic beliefs or values that you hold. In the next column, write behaviors that are consistent with those beliefs. In the final column, list behaviors that are inconsistent with those beliefs. Share your work with the group.

2. Do you have expectations for yourself that are unrealistic or even idealistic?

3. Share some customs you perform simply because of the routine involved, ie, you have always done it that way.

4. Share some things in your past or present that might contribute to an over-active conscience.

5. Are there some things either past or present that you have done to harm others that causes you to feel guilty? Share with the group.

6. Do you ever feel guilty about your relationship with God?

7. How is guilt an expression of God's love?

8. Share ways in which you handle guilt. For example, do you deny it? minimize it? Rationalize it? Seek to justify it? Seek to be perfect?

9. Study and share the activities listed at the end of this chapter.

Chapter 6: From Grief to Release

1. Share an experience involving grief due to loss of someone or something. Describe the feelings you experienced.

2. Record any unsolved issues involving loss. Share these on a voluntary basis. Record ways in which these issues may be resolved.

3. Share ways in which you may actually use grief to fuel addiction.

4. Review the activities at the end of the chapter. Which ones can you use in a meaningful fashion?

Chapter 7: From Resentment to Love

1. What are some ways that you express your anger? Is your anger usually hot or cold?

2. Discuss an experience in which resentment caused you to make a decision you later regretted.

3. Make a list of any resentments you currently harbor. What steps can you take to begin to melt the anger?

4. Review the activities at the end of the chapter. What are the seven steps to use in dealing with resentments?

Chapter 8: From Self-Pity to Gratitude

1. Do you have unrealistic expectations of others? Share some of them or one of them with the group.

2. How do you respond when an expectation is not met?

3. What behaviors and feelings do you exhibit when you are on the "pity pot"?

4. How well do you respond to criticism? When you are being criticized, what feelings emerge?

5. What does the word gratitude mean to you?

6. Review the activities at the end of this chapter. Share with one another.

Chapter 9: From Anxiety to Security

1. Write down and share three things

2. Share an incident from which you made false

projections. For example, you expected things would turn out one way and they actually turned out another way.

3. Can you share a single incident from which worry helped solve a crisis?

4. In what ways are you a people pleaser?

5. Do you ever find yourself withdrawing to avoid anxiety?

6. Relate an incident from which agression resulted with a negative consequence?

7. Review the activities at the end of the chapter. What steps can you begin to take to exhibit more gratitude?

Chapter 10: From Frustration to Serenity

1. Write down and share your three greatest sources of frustration.

2. Share an incident in which frustration was expressed through anger.

3. Share an experience in which you found yourself trying to over-control. Is your desire to control so insatiable that it becomes difficult to identify particular incidents?

4. Would you catergorize yourself as a perfectionist? Have other people ever told you that you were a perfectionist?

5. Do you sometimes seek to manipulate people in order to control them? Do you know other people who do?

6. Has your failure to control ever left you feeling helpless? How did you respond to that feeling?

Chapter 11: From Loneliness to Intimacy

1. Share a time when you felt completely alone.

2. What actions or behaviors have you relied upon in the past to aleviate feelings of loneliness or isolation? What do you do today?

3. Describe ways in which you have masqueraded as someone or something you were not. What feelings accompany this phoniness?

Chapter 12: From Greed to Generosity

1. In what ways do people masquerade ambition for greed? Do you think you have ever done this?

2. Have other people ever told you that you work too hard and too long? Has your work ever interfered with your personal health and social functioning?

3. Review Maslow's heirarchy of needs. Identify things that people do to meet these various needs.

4. What does it mean to covet? How does coveteousness interfere with peace and happiness?

6. What is the relationship between greed and fear?

Chapter 13: From Self-Sufficiency to Grace

1. What is the meaning of grace? How have you experienced grace in your life?

2. Discuss situations in which self-reliance resulted in negative consequences.

3. Share your personal schedule regarding prayer and meditation. Also, share any books, prayers, or other resources that you find helpful.

4. What are some factors in your life which prohibit frequent prayer?

5. What are some ways that you involve yourself with others? How has God used other people to bestow His grace upon you?

6. Discuss how you can used the acronym **D-A-I-L-Y** in your life.

D evote time to meditation

A lways pray

I nvolve yourself with others

L ive the 12 Steps

Y ield yourself to God

Additional Recovery Resources

Books

In Step With God: A Scriptural Guide to 12 Step Programs by Paul Doyle and John Ishee

A concise, penetrating book that provides a biblical basis for the 12 step recovery program.

Prayers for Recovery by Francis Martin.

Prayers you can pray each day as you work your program of recovery.

Audio Tapes

Audio tapes on each chapter of *Spirituality in Recovery* are available from the publisher. These tapes were recorded during a lecture series to recovering persons at Cumberland Heights. Hence, they are not verbatim readings from the book. Rather, they are more spontaneous in nature and supplement the reading material in this book.

Order From:

New Directions, A Division of J M Productions, Inc. P. O. Box 1911, Brentwood, TN 37024-1911. Phone: (615) 373-4814; FAX (615) 373-8495; Toll Free: 800-969-READ.

Epilogue

Step 12 assumes that if you follow the previous steps you will have a spiritual awakening. This awakening may be experienced in a variety of ways. For most people, it is a gradual awareness and commitment. For a few people it is a dramatic experience. Regardless of the nature of the experience, the most important factor is the new relationship that develops as a result of the experience.

We cannot over-emphasize the importance of continued spiritual nurture in the recovery process. What you have begun must be continued if maximum recovery results are to be realized.

There are many way to nurture your spirituality. Several of these were mentioned in Chapter 13. Ultimately, the question arises, What about organized religion? You will hear differing views from various recovering people. It is our contention that involvement in AA *and* a church provide you with the most positive and hopeful approach to spirituality in recovery.

We encourage you to seek God's will in relation to your involvement in a local congregation. You not only need an AA sponsor; you also need a pastor. And, you need people to pray with you and for you, both in AA and in a local congregation.

Additional Recovery Resources

Books

In Step With God: A Scriptural Guide to 12 Step Programs by Paul Doyle and John Ishee

A concise, penetrating book that provides a biblical basis for the 12 step recovery program.

Prayers for Recovery by Francis Martin.

Prayers you can pray each day as you work your program of recovery.

Audio Tapes

Audio tapes on each chapter of *Spirituality in Recovery* are available from the publisher. These tapes were recorded during a lecture series to recovering persons at Cumberland Heights. Hence, they are not verbatim readings from the book. Rather, they are more spontaneous in nature and supplement the reading material in this book.

Order From:

New Directions, A Division of J M Productions, Inc. P. O. Box 1911, Brentwood, TN 37024-1911. Phone: (615) 373-4814; FAX (615) 373-8495; Toll Free: 800-969-READ.